Activities for Lea

RightStart™ Mathematics

by Joan A. Cotter, Ph.D.

LEVEL D
WORKSHEETS

Copyright © 2001 by Joan A. Cotter

All rights reserved. No part of this publication may be reproduced, stored in a retrieval system, or transmitted, in any form or by any means, electronic, mechanical, photocopying, recording, or otherwise, without written permission of Activities for Learning.

The publisher hereby grants permission to reproduce the Worksheets and Practice Sheets for a single child's use.

Printed in the United States of America

www.ALabacus.com

For more information:
info@ALabacus.com

Supplies may be ordered from:
www.ALabacus.com
order@ALabacus.com

Activities for Learning, Inc.
PO Box 468, 321 Hill St.
Hazelton, ND 58544-0468

888-272-3291 or
701-782-2000

fax 701-782-2007

ISBN 978-1-931980-08-1

May 2009

2009

JANUARY
S	M	T	W	T	F	S
				1	2	3
4	5	6	7	8	9	10
11	12	13	14	15	16	17
18	19	20	21	22	23	24
25	26	27	28	29	30	31

FEBRUARY
S	M	T	W	T	F	S
1	2	3	4	5	6	7
8	9	10	11	12	13	14
15	16	17	18	19	20	21
22	23	24	25	26	27	28

MARCH
S	M	T	W	T	F	S
1	2	3	4	5	6	7
8	9	10	11	12	13	14
15	16	17	18	19	20	21
22	23	24	25	26	27	28
29	30	31				

APRIL
S	M	T	W	T	F	S
			1	2	3	4
5	6	7	8	9	10	11
12	13	14	15	16	17	18
19	20	21	22	23	24	25
26	27	28	29	30		

MAY
S	M	T	W	T	F	S
					1	2
3	4	5	6	7	8	9
10	11	12	13	14	15	16
17	18	19	20	21	22	23
24	25	26	27	28	29	30
31						

JUNE
S	M	T	W	T	F	S
	1	2	3	4	5	6
7	8	9	10	11	12	13
14	15	16	17	18	19	20
21	22	23	24	25	26	27
28	29	30				

JULY
S	M	T	W	T	F	S
			1	2	3	4
5	6	7	8	9	10	11
12	13	14	15	16	17	18
19	20	21	22	23	24	25
26	27	28	29	30	31	

AUGUST
S	M	T	W	T	F	S
						1
2	3	4	5	6	7	8
9	10	11	12	13	14	15
16	17	18	19	20	21	22
23	24	25	26	27	28	29
30	31					

SEPTEMBER
S	M	T	W	T	F	S
		1	2	3	4	5
6	7	8	9	10	11	12
13	14	15	16	17	18	19
20	21	22	23	24	25	26
27	28	29	30			

OCTOBER
S	M	T	W	T	F	S
				1	2	3
4	5	6	7	8	9	10
11	12	13	14	15	16	17
18	19	20	21	22	23	24
25	26	27	28	29	30	31

NOVEMBER
S	M	T	W	T	F	S
1	2	3	4	5	6	7
8	9	10	11	12	13	14
15	16	17	18	19	20	21
22	23	24	25	26	27	28
29	30					

DECEMBER
S	M	T	W	T	F	S
		1	2	3	4	5
6	7	8	9	10	11	12
13	14	15	16	17	18	19
20	21	22	23	24	25	26
27	28	29	30	31		

D: © Joan A. Cotter 2005

2010

JANUARY
S	M	T	W	T	F	S
					1	2
3	4	5	6	7	8	9
10	11	12	13	14	15	16
17	18	19	20	21	22	23
24	25	26	27	28	29	30
31						

FEBRUARY
S	M	T	W	T	F	S
	1	2	3	4	5	6
7	8	9	10	11	12	13
14	15	16	17	18	19	20
21	22	23	24	25	26	27
28						

MARCH
S	M	T	W	T	F	S
	1	2	3	4	5	6
7	8	9	10	11	12	13
14	15	16	17	18	19	20
21	22	23	24	25	26	27
28	29	30	31			

APRIL
S	M	T	W	T	F	S
				1	2	3
4	5	6	7	8	9	10
11	12	13	14	15	16	17
18	19	20	21	22	23	24
25	26	27	28	29	30	

MAY
S	M	T	W	T	F	S
						1
2	3	4	5	6	7	8
9	10	11	12	13	14	15
16	17	18	19	20	21	22
23	24	25	26	27	28	29
30	31					

JUNE
S	M	T	W	T	F	S
		1	2	3	4	5
6	7	8	9	10	11	12
13	14	15	16	17	18	19
20	21	22	23	24	25	26
27	28	29	30			

JULY
S	M	T	W	T	F	S
				1	2	3
4	5	6	7	8	9	10
11	12	13	14	15	16	17
18	19	20	21	22	23	24
25	26	27	28	29	30	31

AUGUST
S	M	T	W	T	F	S
1	2	3	4	5	6	7
8	9	10	11	12	13	14
15	16	17	18	19	20	21
22	23	24	25	26	27	28
29	30	31				

SEPTEMBER
S	M	T	W	T	F	S
			1	2	3	4
5	6	7	8	9	10	11
12	13	14	15	16	17	18
19	20	21	22	23	24	25
26	27	28	29	30		

OCTOBER
S	M	T	W	T	F	S
					1	2
3	4	5	6	7	8	9
10	11	12	13	14	15	16
17	18	19	20	21	22	23
24	25	26	27	28	29	30
31						

NOVEMBER
S	M	T	W	T	F	S
	1	2	3	4	5	6
7	8	9	10	11	12	13
14	15	16	17	18	19	20
21	22	23	24	25	26	27
28	29	30				

DECEMBER
S	M	T	W	T	F	S
			1	2	3	4
5	6	7	8	9	10	11
12	13	14	15	16	17	18
19	20	21	22	23	24	25
26	27	28	29	30	31	

D: © Joan A. Cotter 2005

2011

JANUARY

S	M	T	W	T	F	S
						1
2	3	4	5	6	7	8
9	10	11	12	13	14	15
16	17	18	19	20	21	22
23	24	25	26	27	28	29
30	31					

FEBRUARY

S	M	T	W	T	F	S
		1	2	3	4	5
6	7	8	9	10	11	12
13	14	15	16	17	18	19
20	21	22	23	24	25	26
27	28					

MARCH

S	M	T	W	T	F	S
		1	2	3	4	5
6	7	8	9	10	11	12
13	14	15	16	17	18	19
20	21	22	23	24	25	26
27	28	29	30	31		

APRIL

S	M	T	W	T	F	S
					1	2
3	4	5	6	7	8	9
10	11	12	13	14	15	16
17	18	19	20	21	22	23
24	25	26	27	28	29	30

MAY

S	M	T	W	T	F	S
1	2	3	4	5	6	7
8	9	10	11	12	13	14
15	16	17	18	19	20	21
22	23	24	25	26	27	28
29	30	31				

JUNE

S	M	T	W	T	F	S
			1	2	3	4
5	6	7	8	9	10	11
12	13	14	15	16	17	18
19	20	21	22	23	24	25
26	27	28	29	30		

JULY

S	M	T	W	T	F	S
					1	2
3	4	5	6	7	8	9
10	11	12	13	14	15	16
17	18	19	20	21	22	23
24	25	26	27	28	29	30
31						

AUGUST

S	M	T	W	T	F	S
	1	2	3	4	5	6
7	8	9	10	11	12	13
14	15	16	17	18	19	20
21	22	23	24	25	26	27
28	29	30	31			

SEPTEMBER

S	M	T	W	T	F	S
				1	2	3
4	5	6	7	8	9	10
11	12	13	14	15	16	17
18	19	20	21	22	23	24
25	26	27	28	29	30	

OCTOBER

S	M	T	W	T	F	S
						1
2	3	4	5	6	7	8
9	10	11	12	13	14	15
16	17	18	19	20	21	22
23	24	25	26	27	28	29
30	31					

NOVEMBER

S	M	T	W	T	F	S
		1	2	3	4	5
6	7	8	9	10	11	12
13	14	15	16	17	18	19
20	21	22	23	24	25	26
27	28	29	30			

DECEMBER

S	M	T	W	T	F	S
				1	2	3
4	5	6	7	8	9	10
11	12	13	14	15	16	17
18	19	20	21	22	23	24
25	26	27	28	29	30	31

D: © Joan A. Cotter 2005

Game Log

Math Games are an important part of the RightStart™ Mathematics program. Instead of math drills or flashcards, we encourage you to play Math Card Games with the child. The manuals include many games and suggest additional games in the Review and Practice lessons (Levels C to E). For additional games, refer to the *Math Card Games* book.

This game log will help you keep a record of the games you play and when you played them. To help memorization, repetition is essential. Games must be played frequently. Games will help the child practice and apply math skills, especially the facts.

Date	Game Played	Players

© Joan A. Cotter, 2006

Game Log

Date	Game Played	Players
Date	Game Played	Players

Games help children understand, apply, and enjoy mathematics.

© Joan A. Cotter, 2006

Worksheet 1-1, Calendar Problems

Name _____

Date _____

1. How many days are left in this year? Find the answer without counting.

2. How many weeks are in a year? How many weeks are left in this year? If each month had exactly 4 weeks, like February does most of the time, how many months would be in a year?

3. How many days from your birthday this year to your birthday the next year?

4. If a baby is 3 months old, how many days ago was it born?

D: © Joan A. Cotter 2001

Worksheet 1-2, Reviewing Skip Counting

Name _____

Date _____

Write the skip counting patterns for 2.

____ ____ ____ ____ ____

____ ____ ____ ____ ____

Write the skip counting patterns for 4.

____ ____ ____ ____ ____

____ ____ ____ ____ ____

Write the skip counting patterns for 6.

____ ____ ____ ____ ____

____ ____ ____ ____ ____

Write the skip counting patterns for 8.

____ ____ ____ ____ ____

____ ____ ____ ____ ____

Write the skip counting patterns for 9.

____ ____ ____ ____ ____)

____ ____ ____ ____ ____

Write the skip counting patterns for 5.

____ ____

____ ____

____ ____

____ ____

Write the skip counting patterns for 3.

____ ____ ____

____ ____ ____

____ ____ ____

____

Write the skip counting patterns for 7.

____ ____ ____

____ ____ ____

____

D: © Joan A. Cotter 2001

Worksheet 2, Reviewing Addition

Name _____

Date _____

Time _____ Number wrong _____

31 + 7 = _____	98 + 5 = _____	63 + 2 = _____	15 + 2 = _____
39 + 2 = _____	73 + 8 = _____	56 + 3 = _____	33 + 9 = _____
94 + 2 = _____	46 + 8 = _____	28 + 1 = _____	23 + 6 = _____
38 + 9 = _____	52 + 9 = _____	29 + 7 = _____	81 + 8 = _____
48 + 7 = _____	76 + 4 = _____	98 + 3 = _____	88 + 8 = _____
89 + 9 = _____	47 + 9 = _____	15 + 5 = _____	14 + 5 = _____
34 + 8 = _____	65 + 9 = _____	36 + 2 = _____	73 + 4 = _____
59 + 4 = _____	74 + 3 = _____	62 + 6 = _____	66 + 6 = _____
99 + 5 = _____	29 + 8 = _____	41 + 9 = _____	27 + 7 = _____
95 + 6 = _____	22 + 5 = _____	62 + 3 = _____	17 + 2 = _____
87 + 8 = _____	73 + 7 = _____	59 + 1 = _____	61 + 6 = _____
38 + 2 = _____	82 + 8 = _____	24 + 6 = _____	17 + 5 = _____
57 + 4 = _____	47 + 3 = _____	53 + 5 = _____	32 + 7 = _____
91 + 5 = _____	45 + 4 = _____	54 + 4 = _____	82 + 2 = _____
84 + 7 = _____	24 + 9 = _____	48 + 6 = _____	99 + 3 = _____
27 + 6 = _____	73 + 3 = _____	86 + 5 = _____	55 + 7 = _____
16 + 9 = _____	15 + 3 = _____	55 + 8 = _____	82 + 4 = _____
41 + 4 = _____	59 + 6 = _____	58 + 4 = _____	76 + 7 = _____

D: © Joan A. Cotter 2001

Worksheet 3, Addition Practice

Name _____

Date _____

Add the following problem. Explain all you steps as if you were telling another person how and why you do what you do.

```
  946
   78
 +736
```

Add the following problems.

```
   848        4546        6043        5827
  +568       +3874       +3798       +3975
```

```
   541         862         497        5647
   876        4768         972        2976
 +  43       +  90       + 164       + 1234
```

D: © Joan A. Cotter 2001

Worksheet 4, Working With Clocks

Name _____

Date _____

1. Jamie gets on the school bus at 8:05. The ride is a half hour long. What time does Jamie arrive at school?

2. Jamie gets on the bus after school at 3:35. What time does Jamie arrive home?

3. Jay and his family are going to visit his grandmother, who lives an hour and a half away. If they leave at 1:45, what time will they arrive?

4. The next day they leave Jay's grandmother's house at 6:30. What time will they be home?

5. A cuckoo clock just chimed at 12:15. It chimes every quarter hour. Name the next four times it will chime.

6. Joleen finished eating her dinner at 6:30. She went to bed ninety minutes later. What time did she go to bed?

Draw the hands.

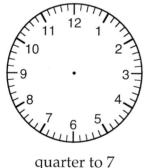

quarter to 7

Draw the hands.

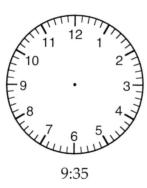

9:35

Write the time two ways.

_____

_____

Fill in the chart.

	3:45	1:20	6:05	9:55
1 hour later	4:45			
30 minutes later	4:15			
5 minutes later				

D: © Joan A. Cotter 2001

Worksheet 5, Perimeter in Inches

Name _____

Date _____

1. Show the inch marks and write the measurements. One side is done. Then find the perimeter of the rectangle in inches. Use equations.

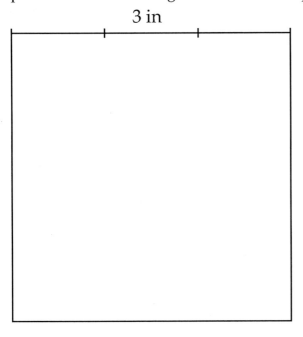

3 in

2. Find the perimeter of the rectangle in inches. Show the inch marks and measurements.

3. Find the perimeter of this sheet of paper in inches.

D: © Joan A. Cotter 2001

Worksheet 6-A, Review

Name _____

Date _____

1. Write only the answers to the oral questions. _____ _____ _____

4. Write only the answers. 85 + 25 = _____   63 + 58 = _____   125 + 15 = _____

7. Draw the hands.   Draw the hands.   Write the time two ways.

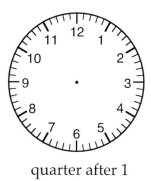
quarter after 1

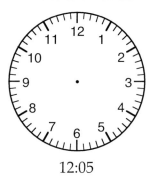
12:05

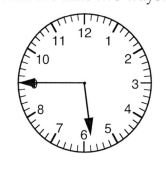
_____

_____

11. Write the first three months of the year. How many days are in those months?

12. Add 467 + 28 + 3165.

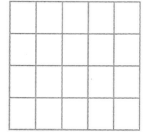

13. Write the multiples of 3. Circle the even numbers.

____ ____ ____

____ ____ ____

____ ____ ____

____

D: © Joan A. Cotter 2001

Worksheet 6-B, Review

Name _____

Date _____

1. Write only the answers to the oral questions. _____ _____ _____

4. Write only the answers. 96 + 34 = _____   47 + 74 = _____   136 + 14 = _____

7. Draw the hands.   Draw the hands.   Write the time two ways.

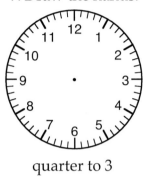
quarter to 3

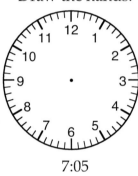
7:05

_____

_____

11. Write the last three months of the year. How many days are in those months?

12. Add 74 + 2388 + 19.

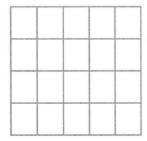

13. Write the multiples of 5. Circle the even numbers.

_____ _____

_____ _____

_____ _____

_____ _____

_____ _____

D: © Joan A. Cotter 2001

Worksheet 7, Perimeter in Feet and Inches

Name _____

Date _____

1. Take two pieces of construction paper and measure them in feet and inches. Write the measurements on the figures below. Then find the perimeters.

2. Write your height in inches and in feet and inches.

_____

3. On Monday Marc walked around this block. How far did he walk? Was it a mile? A mile is 5280 feet.

569 ft

687 ft

4. On Tuesday Mary walked around this block. How far did she walk? Who walked farther, Mary or Marc, and how much farther?

596 ft

658 ft

D: © Joan A. Cotter 2001

Worksheet 8, Perimeters With Fractions

Name _____

Date _____

1. Divide the rectangle into fourths. Color one of the fourths and find its perimeter.

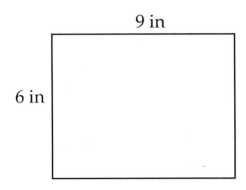

2. Divide the rectangle into fourths a different way. Color one of the fourths and find its perimeter.

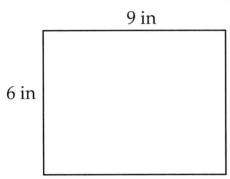

3. Divide the rectangle into fourths a different way. Color one of the fourths and find its perimeter.

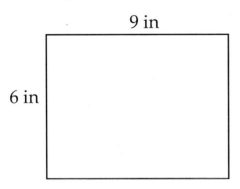

4. Find the perimeter of the rectangle.

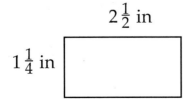

D: © Joan A. Cotter 2001

Worksheet 9, Quarters of an Hour

Name _____

Date _____

Explain how you found your answers to the problems.

1. Jay and Kay ride the school bus. The trip takes a quarter of an hour. How much time do they spend on the bus in a week?

2. Carlos and Kendra watch TV an hour and a half every day. How many hours do they watch in a week?

3. The third grade class is going on a field trip to a farm, which is three quarters of an hour away. They are supposed to be there at 10:00. They leave at 9:30. Will they arrive on time? How early or late will they be?

4. Some people, especially business people, divide the months of the year into quarters. Write the months for each quarter.

First Quarter	Second Quarter	Third Quarter	Fourth Quarter

5. Which quarter has the greatest number of days?

D: © Joan A. Cotter 2001

Worksheet 10, Fractions of a Dollar

Name _____

Date _____

Write the values and names of the fractions of a dollar.

1 $\underline{100¢}$			
$\underline{\text{dollar}}$			
$\frac{1}{2}$ _____ _____		$\frac{1}{2}$ _____ _____	
$\frac{1}{4}$ _____ _____	$\frac{1}{4}$ _____ _____	$\frac{1}{4}$ _____ _____	$\frac{1}{4}$ _____ _____
$\frac{1}{10}$ ___ $\frac{1}{10}$ ___ $\frac{1}{10}$ ___ $\frac{1}{10}$ ___ $\frac{1}{10}$ ___	$\frac{1}{10}$ ___ $\frac{1}{10}$ ___	$\frac{1}{10}$ ___ $\frac{1}{10}$ ___	$\frac{1}{10}$ ___ $\frac{1}{10}$ ___

1. How many quarters equal a dollar? _____

2. How many quarters are equal to 2 dollars? _____

3. How many dimes are equal to a dollar? _____

4. How many pennies in a dollar and a half? _____

5. Which is greater, 3 quarters or 1 dollar? _____

6. How much does 2 quarters equal? _____

7. How many quarters are in a dollar and a half? _____

8. How many dimes are equal to half a dollar? _____

9. Which is greater, 6 quarters or 3 half dollars? _____

10. If half a pizza costs a dollar and a half, what does a whole pizza cost? _____

D: © Joan A. Cotter 2001

Worksheet 11-A, Review

Name _____

Date _____

1. Write only the answers to the oral questions. _____ _____ _____

4. Write only the answers. 75 + 19 = _____   47 + 26 = _____   81 + 24 = _____

7. Write the fractions in the rectangles.

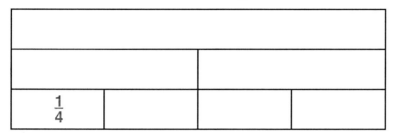

13. Show $3\frac{1}{2}$ inches on the ruler. Circle or shade it.

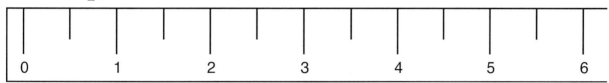

14. How many minutes in a quarter of an hour? _____

15. How many minutes in three quarters of an hour? _____

16. How much money is a quarter of a dollar? _____

17. How much money is three quarters of a dollar? _____

18. How much is half of $4\frac{1}{2}$ inches? _____

36. Add 637 + 6456.

19. Write the first 15 multiples of 2.

_____ _____ _____ _____ _____

_____ _____ _____ _____ _____

_____ _____ _____ _____ _____

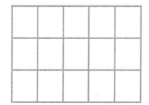

35. What patterns do you see in the multiples of 2?

D: © Joan A. Cotter 2001

Worksheet 11-B, Review

Name

Date _____

1. Write only the answers to the oral questions. _____ _____ _____

4. Write only the answers. 16 + 76 = _____   53 + 38 = _____   87 + 24 = _____

7. Write the fractions in the rectangles.

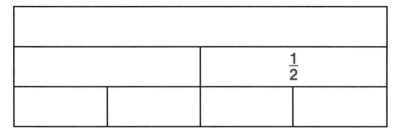

13. Show $4\frac{1}{2}$ inches on the ruler. Circle or shade it.

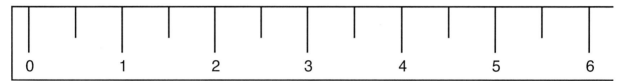

14. How much money is a quarter of a dollar? _____

15. How much money is four quarters of a dollar? _____

16. How many minutes in a quarter of an hour? _____

17. How many minutes in four quarters of an hour? _____

18. How much is half of $6\frac{1}{2}$ inches? _____

36. Add 729 + 8576.

19. Write the first 15 multiples of 2.

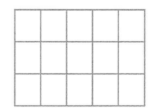

___ ___ ___ ___ ___

___ ___ ___ ___ ___

___ ___ ___ ___ ___

35. What patterns do you see in the multiples of 2?

D: © Joan A. Cotter 2001

Worksheet 12, Money as Fractions

Name _____

Date _____

1. Use crosshatching to show adding 8 dimes plus 9 dimes. Write the equation.

$ dollar										$ dollar									
d	d	d	d	d	d	d	d	d	d	d	d	d	d	d	d	d	d	d	d

_____

2. Use crosshatching to show adding 6 pennies plus 7 pennies. Write the equations.

dime										dime									
p	p	p	p	p	p	p	p	p	p	p	p	p	p	p	p	p	p	p	p

_____

_____

Write these sums using a dollar sign.

3. 0 dollars   9 dimes   6 pennies _____

4. 0 dollars   13 dimes   5 pennies _____

5. 1 dollars   4 dimes   16 pennies _____

6. 0 dollars   8 dimes   20 pennies _____

7. 2 dollars   12 dimes   20 pennies _____

8. 1 dollars   20 dimes   20 pennies _____

9. 1 dollars   0 dimes   200 pennies _____

10. 0 dollars   100 dimes   0 pennies _____

11. 3 dollars   90 dimes   100 pennies _____

12. 0 dollars   5 dimes   150 pennies _____

D: © Joan A. Cotter 2001

Worksheet 13, Making Change Different Ways

Name _____

Date _____

Crosshatch on the chart a way to make 25¢, using at least 4 coins.

quarter				
dime		dime		
nickel	nickel	nickel	nickel	nickel
p p p p p	p p p p p	p p p p p	p p p p p	p p p p p

Find all the ways to make 25¢. Use some kind of order to find them.

____ quarters ____ dimes ____ nickels ____ pennies

____ quarters ____ dimes ____ nickels ____ pennies

____ quarters ____ dimes ____ nickels ____ pennies

____ quarters ____ dimes ____ nickels ____ pennies

____ quarters ____ dimes ____ nickels ____ pennies

____ quarters ____ dimes ____ nickels ____ pennies

____ quarters ____ dimes ____ nickels ____ pennies

____ quarters ____ dimes ____ nickels ____ pennies

____ quarters ____ dimes ____ nickels ____ pennies

____ quarters ____ dimes ____ nickels ____ pennies

____ quarters ____ dimes ____ nickels ____ pennies

____ quarters ____ dimes ____ nickels ____ pennies

____ quarters ____ dimes ____ nickels ____ pennies

D: © Joan A. Cotter 2001

Worksheet 14, Gallons and Quarts

Name _____

Date _____

Write the names and values of the fractions of a gallon.

gallon	
$\frac{1}{2}$ _____	__ _____
__ _____	__ _____	__ _____	__ _____

Write =, <, or > in the circles.

a. 4 quarts ◯ 1 gallon   f. 6 quarts ◯ 2 gallons

b. 1 half gallon ◯ 1 quart   g. 1 half gallon ◯ 2 quarts

c. 1 gallon ◯ 3 quarts   h. $\frac{1}{2}$ gallon ◯ 1 quart

d. 2 quarts ◯ 2 half gallons   i. 10 quarts ◯ 10 gallons

e. $\frac{1}{4}$ gallon ◯ 1 quart   j. 3 gallons ◯ 12 quarts

One quart is equal to 32 ounces.

k. How many ounces in two quarts? _____

l. How many ounces in a half gallon? _____

m. How many ounces in 2 half gallons? _____

n. How many ounces in a gallon? _____

o. How many ounces in a half gallon plus a quart? _____

D: © Joan A. Cotter 2001

Worksheet 15, Gallon Problems

Name _____

Date _____

gallon				
half gallon			half gallon	
quart	quart	quart	quart	

1. Ms Black wants to buy a gallon of milk. Which is the cheapest way for her to buy it— gallon, half gallons, or quarts? Use the chart below for the prices. Explain your work.

gallon	$2.98
half gallon	$1.54
quart	$0.78

2. Mr. Black wants to buy exactly 2 gallons of ice cream. He wants to buy 3 different flavors, vanilla, chocolate, and strawberry. He can buy it in gallon, half gallon, and quart containers. What are all the different ways he can buy it?

D: © Joan A. Cotter 2001

Worksheet 16, Musical Notes

Name _____

Date _____

1. Write the notes and their names in the chart below. Also write the number of beats.

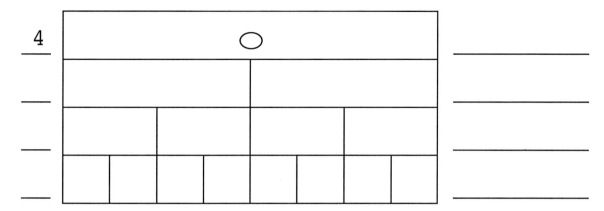

2. Draw notes to complete the measures. Draw a note on each line.

D: © Joan A. Cotter 2001

Worksheet 17-A, Review

Name _____

Date _____

1. Write only the answers to the oral questions. _____ _____ _____

4. Write only the answers. 64 + 36 = _____   58 + 39 = _____   76 + 28 = _____

7. How many minutes are in two quarters of an hour? _____

8. What do we call one fourth of a gallon? _____

9. What do we call one fourth of a dollar? _____

10. What do we call one fourth of a whole note in music? _____

11. How much money is three halves of a dollar? _____

12. How much is half of $8\frac{1}{2}$ inches? _____

13. Jill is 3 feet 9 inches tall. Jack is 6 inches taller than Jill. How tall is Jack? (Remember that 1 foot equals 12 inches.)

14. Chris has 9 quarters and 4 dimes. How much money does Chris have altogether?

15. Write the multiples of 6.

____ ____ ____ ____ ____

____ ____ ____ ____ ____

25. Add $17.89 + $9.37.

D: © Joan A. Cotter 2001

Worksheet 17-B, Review

Name _____

Date _____

1. Write only the answers to the oral questions. _____   _____   _____

4. Write only the answers. 27 + 73 = _____   67 + 58 = _____   38 + 84 = _____

7. How many minutes are in three quarters of an hour? _____

8. What do we call one fourth of a gallon? _____

9. What do we call one fourth of a dollar? _____

10. What do we call one fourth of a whole note in music? _____

11. How much money is two halves of a dollar? _____

12. How much is half of $10\frac{1}{2}$ inches? _____

13. Ray is 3 feet 10 inches tall. Rachel is 4 inches taller than Ray. How tall is Rachel? (Remember that 1 foot equals 12 inches.)

14. Jordan has 7 quarters and 6 nickels. How much money does Jordan have altogether?

15. Write the multiples of 6.

_____ _____ _____ _____ _____

_____ _____ _____ _____ _____

25. Add $9.65 + $16.75.

D: © Joan A. Cotter 2001

Worksheet 18, Right Angles and Degrees

Name _____

Date _____

What kind of lines are in the equals sign. _____

What kind of lines are in the plus sign. _____

How many degrees are in a right angle? _____   Circle the right angles below.

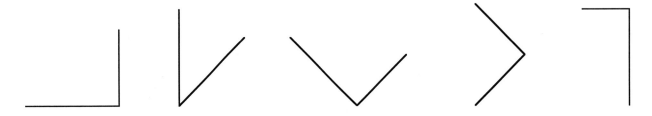

Write the capital letters of the alphabet that have right angles. _____

Fill in the blanks. The symbol for degree is °.

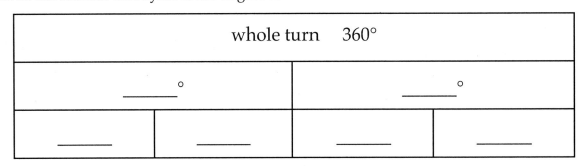

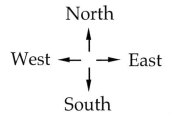

If you are facing east and turn right 90°, what direction will you be facing? _____

If you are facing west and turn right 90°, what direction will you be facing? _____

If you are facing north and turn left 180°, what direction will you be facing? _____

If you are facing south and turn right 270°, what direction will you be facing? _____

If you are facing east and turn right 360°, what direction will you be facing? _____

D: © Joan A. Cotter 2001

Worksheet 19, Skip Counting Patterns

Name _____

Date _____

Fill in the missing blanks.

2	4	6	8	10
1_	1_	1_	1_	20

4	8	_2	_6	_0
_4	_8	_2	_6	_0

6	1_	1_	2_	3_
3_	4_	4_	5_	60

8	1_	2_	3_	4_
4_	5_	6_	7_	8_

_	_	_
1_	1_	1_
2_	2_	2_
30		

_	1_	2_
2_	3_	4_
4_	5_	6_
70		

5	_0
1_	_0
2_	_0
3_	_0
4_	_0

9	1_	2_	3_	4_
9_	8_	7_	6_	5_

Which multiples have all even numbers? _____

Which multiples have all odd numbers? _____

In which multiple do the ones count by twos backward? _____

In which multiple is the second row 30 more than the first row? _____

In which multiple is the difference between numbers next to each other always 7? _____

In which multiples are all the numbers from 0 to 9 used in the ones place? _____

In which multiple do the digits always add up to 9? _____

D: © Joan A. Cotter 2001

Worksheet 20, Multiplying with Multiples

Name _____

Date _____

Use the multiples table to find the answers and circle the numbers in the tables.

4 taken 3 times = _____   4 taken 6 times = _____

4	8	12	16	20
24	28	32	36	40

4 × 3 = _____   4 × 6 = _____

4 taken 8 times = _____   4 × 9 = _____

4 × 8 = _____   4 × 4 = _____

7 taken 3 times = _____   7 × 2 = _____

7	14	21
28	35	42
49	56	63
70		

7 × 3 = _____   7 × 7 = _____

7 × 6 = _____   7 × 4 = _____

7 × 9 = _____   7 × 5 = _____

Use the multiples tables to find the answers.

2	4	6	8	10
12	14	16	18	20

3	6	9
12	15	18
21	24	27
30		

8	16	24	32	40
48	56	64	72	80

6	12	18	24	30
36	42	48	54	60

9	18	27	36	45
90	81	72	63	54

2 × 8 = _____   8 × 9 = _____   6 × 4 = _____

3 × 6 = _____   3 × 1 = _____   8 × 6 = _____

8 × 4 = _____   9 × 4 = _____   3 × 8 = _____

9 × 3 = _____   6 × 6 = _____   9 × 8 = _____

Write equations for the circled numbers using 8s.

8	16	(24)	32	40
48	(56)	64	72	80

_____

_____

D: © Joan A. Cotter 2001

Worksheet 21, Adding the Same Number

Name _____

Find the sums.

Date _____

```
 3    3    3    3    3    3    3    3    3
+3    3    3    3    3    3    3    3    3
     +3    3    3    3    3    3    3    3
          +3    3    3    3    3    3    3
               +3    3    3    3    3    3
                    +3    3    3    3    3
                         +3    3    3    3
                              +3    3    3
                                   +3    3
                                        +3
```

Chris soon will be 8 years old. How many days old will Chris be on that birthday?

```
 4    4    4    4    4    4    4    4    4
+4    4    4    4    4    4    4    4    4
     +4    4    4    4    4    4    4    4
          +4    4    4    4    4    4    4
               +4    4    4    4    4    4
                    +4    4    4    4    4
                         +4    4    4    4
                              +4    4    4
                                   +4    4
                                        +4
```

What pattern do you see?

Add the following numbers. Use skip counting multiples to find the sums.

```
   72      25     819     405     333      97
   72      25     819     405     333      97
   72      25     819     405     333      97
   72      25   + 819     405     333      97
   72      25            405     333      97
   72      25            405     333      97
   72      25            405   + 333      97
 + 72    + 25          + 405             97
                                          97
                                        + 97
```

D: © Joan A. Cotter 2001

Worksheet 22, Continuing Geometric Patterns

Name _____

Date _____

Continue the pattern with one more term.

Worksheet 23-A, Review

Name _____

Date _____

1. Write only the answers to the oral questions. _____ _____ _____

4. Write only the answers.   56 + 14 = _____   39 + 29 = _____   67 + 98 = _____

7. Write the multiples of 8.

___ ___ ___ ___ ___

___ ___ ___ ___ ___

17. Jan and Jay are buying trees to plant. Each tree costs $3.89. How much will eight trees cost?

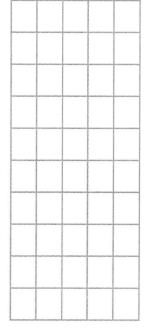

18. Draw $7\frac{1}{2}$ cookies.

19. Draw a right angle. How many degrees does it have?

21. A quart holds 32 ounces. How many ounces are in a half gallon? How many ounces in a gallon?

23. Jan and Jay plant five trees. Each tree takes them a quarter of an hour. If they start at 9:15, what time will they finish?

24. How many minutes is 5 quarters of an hour?

25. How much money is 5 quarters of a dollar?

D: © Joan A. Cotter 2001

Worksheet 23-B, Review

Name _____

Date _____

1. Write only the answers to the oral questions. _____ _____ _____

4. Write only the answers.   73 + 17 = _____   47 + 49 = _____   78 + 99 = _____

7. Write the multiples of 9.

____ ____ ____ ____ ____

____ ____ ____ ____ ____

17. Jordan is buying lilac bushes to plant. Each bush costs $4.79. How much will nine bushes cost?

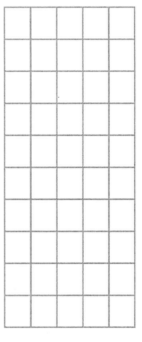

18. Draw $6\frac{1}{2}$ cookies.

19. Draw a right angle. How many degrees does it have?

21. A quart holds 4 cups. How many cups are in a half gallon? How many cups in a gallon?

23. Jordan is planting 6 lilac bushes on Monday. Each takes a quarter of an hour. If Jordan starts at 9:30, what time will Jordan finish?

24. How many minutes is 3 quarters of an hour?

25. How much money is 6 quarters of a dollar?

D: © Joan A. Cotter 2001

Worksheet 24, Continuing Numeric Patterns

Name _____

Date _____

Write the next two terms for each pattern.

35	37	39	_____	_____
102	101	100	_____	_____
9	18	27	_____	_____
16	24	32	_____	_____
35	30	25	_____	_____
18	24	30	_____	_____
3	6	9	_____	_____
3	6	12	_____	_____
4	40	400	_____	_____
80	40	20	_____	_____
1	4	9	_____	_____
0¢	25¢	50¢	_____	_____
$0.05	$0.10	$0.15	_____	_____
$0.01	$0.10	$1.00	_____	_____
$1.00	$1.50	$2.00	_____	_____
1	$1\frac{1}{2}$	2	_____	_____
0	$\frac{1}{4}$	$\frac{1}{2}$	_____	_____
5	$4\frac{1}{2}$	4	_____	_____
$\frac{1}{2}$	$\frac{1}{3}$	$\frac{1}{4}$	_____	_____

D: © Joan A. Cotter 2001

Worksheet 25, Subtracting by Going Up

Name _____

Date _____

Solve the addition equations and rewrite them as subtraction equations.

6 + ___ = 10 _____

8 + ___ = 20 _____

27 + ___ = 31 _____

46 + ___ = 53 _____

39 + ___ = 48 _____

___ + 9 = 17 _____

___ + 17 = 24 _____

___ + 12 = 30 _____

___ + 26 = 35 _____

___ + 51 = 62 _____

Solve these subtraction equations by going up.

39 − 33 = ___   50 − 32 = ___

31 − 28 = ___   62 − 49 = ___

13 − 8 = ___   79 − 62 = ___

74 − 71 = ___   100 − 82 = ___

51 − 31 = ___   101 − 92 = ___

105 − 96 = ___   41 − 23 = ___

75 − 50 = ___   56 − 39 = ___

Explain how to find 64 − 48.

D: © Joan A. Cotter 2001

Worksheet 26, Reviewing Subtraction Facts ≤ 10

Name _____

Date _____

8 – 6 = ___	8 – 5 = ___	10 – 2 = ___	9 – 7 = ___	8 – 7 = ___
3 – 2 = ___	6 – 2 = ___	10 – 8 = ___	8 – 2 = ___	10 – 9 = ___
9 – 4 = ___	9 – 6 = ___	6 – 1 = ___	9 – 8 = ___	9 – 2 = ___
6 – 4 = ___	2 – 1 = ___	8 – 4 = ___	9 – 3 = ___	6 – 5 = ___
7 – 3 = ___	7 – 6 = ___	5 – 4 = ___	8 – 3 = ___	8 – 1 = ___
9 – 5 = ___	10 – 7 = ___	9 – 1 = ___	5 – 3 = ___	10 – 1 = ___
10 – 3 = ___	7 – 2 = ___	10 – 4 = ___	3 – 1 = ___	4 – 2 = ___
10 – 5 = ___	5 – 2 = ___	7 – 5 = ___	6 – 3 = ___	4 – 3 = ___
4 – 1 = ___	7 – 1 = ___	10 – 6 = ___	5 – 1 = ___	7 – 4 = ___

10	8	3	10	6	4	6	8	5
–1	–4	–2	–5	–1	–3	–3	–2	–1

10	5	10	9	3	9	7	9	8
–7	–2	–3	–2	–1	–1	–5	–7	–1

10	9	6	10	7	8	7	4	7
–2	–8	–2	–4	–6	–7	–1	–2	–3

9	6	7	8	2	9	10	7	8
–6	–4	–4	–6	–1	–3	–6	–2	–5

5	10	9	8	10	9	5	4	6
–4	–9	–4	–3	–8	–5	–3	–1	–5

D: © Joan A. Cotter 2001

Worksheet 27, Reviewing Subtraction Facts >10

Name _____

Date _____

12 – 8 = ____   16 – 7 = ____   11 – 5 = ____   12 – 7 = ____   13 – 9 = ____

15 – 8 = ____   14 – 5 = ____   13 – 7 = ____   12 – 9 = ____   15 – 7 = ____

14 – 9 = ____   11 – 9 = ____   16 – 8 = ____   11 – 7 = ____   11 – 2 = ____

14 – 8 = ____   15 – 6 = ____   13 – 6 = ____   12 – 5 = ____   11 – 8 = ____

14 – 7 = ____   12 – 3 = ____   14 – 6 = ____   17 – 8 = ____   16 – 9 = ____

11 – 6 = ____   11 – 3 = ____   12 – 6 = ____   13 – 8 = ____   13 – 4 = ____

15 – 9 = ____   13 – 5 = ____   12 – 4 = ____   17 – 9 = ____   11 – 4 = ____

18 – 9 = ____

12 −6	13 −5	11 −3	13 −7	14 −8	11 −2	12 −9	14 −5	13 −9
12 −5	12 −8	13 −4	11 −6	15 −9	12 −4	13 −8	11 −4	15 −6
14 −6	12 −3	18 −9	15 −8	12 −7	14 −9	11 −8	14 −7	11 −9
13 −6	17 −8	16 −8	11 −5	16 −9	15 −7	11 −7	17 −9	16 −7

Give two ways for finding 11 – 8.

D: © Joan A. Cotter 2001

Worksheet 28-A, Review

Name _____

Date _____

1. Write only the answers to the oral questions. _____ _____ _____

4. Write only the answers.   56 – 51 = _____   61 – 3 = _____   32 – 10 = _____

7. Write the multiples of 8.

___ ___ ___ ___ ___

___ ___ ___ ___ ___

17. How much is four 8s? _____

18. How much is ten 8s? _____

19. How much is eight 8s? _____

20. How much is six 8s? _____

21. How much is one 8? _____

22. What is perimeter?

_____

_____

23. Circle the angles that are 90°. What is another name for these angles? _____

25. Draw $3\frac{1}{4}$ pizzas.

26. Nathan spends 55 minutes every day in math class. How many minutes is that in a week?

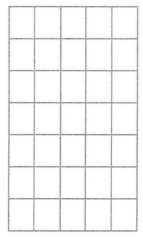

27. What strategy could you use to find 15 – 9 if you didn't know it?

D: © Joan A. Cotter 2001

Worksheet 28-B, Review

Name _____

Date _____

1. Write only the answers to the oral questions. _____ _____ _____

4. Write only the answers.   76 – 42 = _____   32 – 4 = _____   57 – 10 = _____

7. Write the multiples of 6.

_____ _____ _____ _____ _____

_____ _____ _____ _____ _____

22. What is perimeter?

_____

_____

17. How much is three 6s? _____

18. How much is six 6s? _____

19. How much is ten 6s? _____

20. How much is four 6s? _____

21. How much is one 6? _____

23. Circle the angles that are 90°. What is another name for these angles? _____

   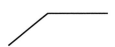

25. Draw $1\frac{1}{4}$ pizzas.

26. Natalie spends 45 minutes every day in math class. How many minutes is that in a week?

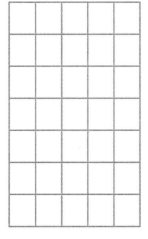

27. What strategy could you use to find 16 – 9 if you didn't know it?

D: © Joan A. Cotter 2001

Worksheet 29, Adding Hours and Minutes

Name _____

Date _____

1. Alberto wanted to know how long it took him to build a model. The first day he worked 2 hours and 20 minutes. The second day he worked 1 hour and 45 minutes and finished it. How long did it take him?

2. Anna is building a different model. She spent 1 hour 45 minutes for three days. How long did it take her?

3. Amelia practices her violin for 25 minutes each day except Sunday. How much time does she practice in a week?

4. Adam practices the piano 35 minutes five days a week. How much time does he practice in a week?

```
  4 hr 15 min              3 hr 29 min
+ 5 hr 48 min              3 hr 29 min
                         + 3 hr 29 min
```

D: © Joan A. Cotter 2001

Worksheet 30, Subtracting Hours and Minutes

Name _____

Date _____

1. Jane is attending a play that lasts 2 hours and 10 minutes. She has been watching the play for 1 hour and 35 minutes. How soon will it be over?

2. Jon sleeps 9 hours and 45 minutes a day. How many hours is he awake in a day?

3. Jack and Jill built a birdhouse together. It took them 4 hours and 5 minutes. Jill spent 2 hours and 15 minutes. How much time did Jack spend?

4. Jay skied for 3 hours and 45 minutes. Jean skied 4 hours and 20 minutes. Who skied more and how much more?

a.   3 hr 10 min
     − 2 hr 20 min

b.   3 hr 35 min
     −   45 min

c.   5 hr 10 min
     − 2 hr 45 min

d.   24 hr   0 min
     − 20 hr 52 min

e.   5 hr 18 min
     − 1 hr 38 min

f.   10 hr 25 min
     − 7 hr 17 min

D: © Joan A. Cotter 2001

Worksheet 31, Trading Between Inches and Feet

Name _____

Date _____

1. The height of the ceiling in many homes is 8 ft. How many inches is that?

2. Robert is building a square pen for his pet rabbit. One side measures 2 ft 9 in. What is the perimeter? If the rabbit walks next to the fence all the way around the pen, how far would it walk? Draw a picture of the pen.

3. Charlotte is 4 feet 2 inches tall. Her little brother, Charles, is 2 feet 10 inches tall. How much taller is Charlotte?

4. Work with your partner and measure each other. How tall are you in feet and inches? How tall are you in inches? Show your work.

a. 4 ft 7 in.
  + 4 ft 7 in.

b. 3 ft 4 in.
    3 ft 4 in.
  + 3 ft 4 in.

c. 8 ft 4 in.
  − 3 ft 5 in.

d. 5 ft 8 in.
  − 1 ft 10 in.

D: © Joan A. Cotter 2001

Worksheet 32, Place Value Names

Name _____

Date _____

Write these mixed-up numbers in the correct order. The numbers are in the boxes along the right. Cross them out as you use them.

a. 3 tens 2 ones 5 hundreds _____

b. 4 hundreds 2 tens 2 ones 3 thousands _____

c. 5 tens 3 thousands 6 hundreds 4 ones _____

d. 5 ones 2 thousands _____

e. 5 ones 4 tens 3 hundreds _____

f. 2 hundreds 4 tens 3 thousands _____

g. 3 thousands 2 tens 4 ones 3 hundreds _____

h. 5 hundreds 2 ones 3 thousands _____

i. 2 tens 3 ones 2 thousands _____

345
3240
3422
3654
2023
3324
2005
532
3502

Explain how you can get the new number on your calculator without clearing it. You can use adding or subtracting, but tell how much. Try it to be sure.

j. Enter 6124 and change the number to 6120. _____

k. Enter 4638 and change the number to 4038. _____

l. Enter 1503 and change the number to 1593. _____

m. Enter 9046 and change the number to 9346. _____

n. Enter 3072 and change the number to 72. _____

o. Enter 3300 and change the number to 3399. _____

p. Enter 4006 and change the number to 4446. _____

D: © Joan A. Cotter 2001

Worksheet 33, Place Value Problems

Name _____

Date _____

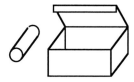

1. A certain candy, called Lime Favors, is wrapped with ten in a roll. How many pieces of candy are in 36 rolls?

2. Ten rolls of Lime Favors fit in a box. Pat has 300 pieces of candy. How many rolls can Pat make? How many boxes can Pat fill?

3. One box of Lime Favors has 6 whole rolls and 18 pieces of candy from broken rolls. How many pieces of candy are in the box?

4. Another box of Lime Favors has 7 whole rolls and 13 pieces of candy. How many pieces are needed to fill the box?

a. 100 = _____ ones

b. 200 = _____ ones

c. 110 = _____ tens

d. 180 = _____ tens

e. 100 = _____ hundreds

f. 200 = _____ hundreds

g. 5 tens + 17 ones = _____

h. 4 tens + 19 ones = _____

i. 83 = 7 tens + _____ ones

j. 71 = 6 tens + _____ ones

k. 38 = _____ tens + 8 ones

l. 38 = _____ tens + 18 ones

m. 43 tens = 4 hundreds + _____ tens

n. 97 tens = 9 hundreds + _____ tens

D: © Joan A. Cotter 2001

Worksheet 34-A, Review

Name _____

Date _____

1. Write only the answers to the oral questions. _____ _____ _____

4. Write only the answers. 64 − 41 = _____   72 − 23 = _____   95 − 27 = _____

7. Write the multiples of 6.

____ ____ ____ ____ ____

____ ____ ____ ____ ____

10. How much is three 6s? _____

11. How much is five 6s? _____

12. How much is ten 6s? _____

13. How much is seven 6s? _____

14. How much is eight 6s? _____

15. This line is 1 inch long. ⊢——⊣
Draw a line $2\frac{1}{2}$ inches long.

17. Write this mixed-up number using digits 0 to 9.

8 hundred 6 ones 9 thousand

_____

16. Explain how you can tell how many squares there are without counting past 10.

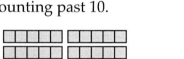

18. The Garcia family is traveling to see the grandparents. They drove 2 hours and 45 minutes before a stop and 1 hour 45 minutes after the stop. How long was the drive?

19. Chris entered 4972 on a calculator. How could Chris change the number to read 4072 without clearing the calculator?

_____

20.

10	11	13	10	16
−4	−4	−6	−7	−8

25.

9	17	13
−3	−8	−5

D: © Joan A. Cotter 2001

Worksheet 34-B, Review

Name _____

Date _____

1. Write only the answers to the oral questions. _____ _____ _____

4. Write only the answers. 87 − 33 = _____   66 − 9 = _____   84 − 36 = _____

7. Write the multiples of 8.

____ ____ ____ ____ ____

____ ____ ____ ____ ____

10. How much is eight 8s? _____

11. How much is three 8s? _____

12. How much is six 8s? _____

13. How much is seven 8s? _____

14. How much is five 8s? _____

15. This line is 1 inch long. ├────┤
Draw a line $1\frac{1}{2}$ inches long.

16. Explain how you can tell how many squares there are without counting past 10.

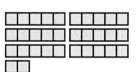

17. Write this mixed-up number using digits 0 to 9.

3 thousands 4 ones 7 tens

_____

18. The Silver family is traveling to see an aunt and uncle. It takes 5 hours and to drive. They drove 2 hours and 45 minutes before a stop. How much longer do they need to drive?

19. Jamie entered 8057 on a calculator. How could Jamie change the number to read 8007 without clearing the calculator?

_____

20.
```
 10    11    14    11    17     9    16    12
− 3   − 3   − 6   − 7   − 8   − 4   − 9   − 4
```
25.

D: © Joan A. Cotter 2001

Worksheet 35, Adding & Subtracting by Compensating

Name _____

Date _____

Change the numbers to make these problems easier.
Write the new equation and the answer on the lines.

1. 42 + 38 = _
   40 + 40 = ____

2. 16 + 14 = _
   ____

3. 52 + 49 = _
   ____

4. 298 + 198 = _
   ____

5. 64 − 29 = _
   ____

6. 32 − 19 = _
   ____

7. 55 − 28 = _
   ____

8. 60 − 18 = _
   ____

9. 130 − 99 = _
   ____

10. 579 − 99 = _
    ____

11. 267 − 198 = _
    ____

12. 378 − 190 = _
    ____

Worksheet 36, Multidigit Subtraction

Name _____

Date _____

```
  8445        2149        7141        6632
− 5372      − 1524      − 5308      − 4059
```

```
  2159        3162        9468        8277
−  451      − 1094      − 4585      − 5549
```

D: © Joan A. Cotter 2001

Worksheet 37, Checking Subtraction by Adding

Name _____

Date _____

Find the correct subtraction problem by adding. Then circle the correct answer.

```
   8272         8272         8272
 - 3446       - 3446       - 3446
   ————         ————         ————
   5826         5836         4826


   7505         7505         7505
 - 1371       - 1371       - 1371
   ————         ————         ————
   6174         6134         6274


   2642         2642         2642
 - 1295       - 1295       - 1295
   ————         ————         ————
   1447         1357         1347


   7129         7129         7129
 - 2736       - 2736       - 2736
   ————         ————         ————
   4393         4493         4383


   9513         9513         9513
 - 7885       - 7885       - 7885
   ————         ————         ————
   1728         1628         1638
```

D: © Joan A. Cotter 2001

Worksheet 38, Subtracting With Doubles and Zeroes

Name _____

Date _____

Subtract and check.

```
  8344      6188      5628      6686
- 2381    - 5686    - 2643    - 6589
```

```
  5819      7291      9605      8800
- 4949    - 1799    - 3609    - 4981
```

```
  5613      9721      8272      7581
- 5424    - 3354    - 5579    - 4515
```

```
  5128      9805      7447      9720
- 1837    - 5890    - 1589    - 2364
```

```
  6062      3900      8488      8000
- 4263    -  865    - 4789    -   89
```

D: © Joan A. Cotter 2001

Worksheet 39, Using Check Numbers

Name _____

Date _____

Check Number Table

1 (1)	2 (2)	3 (3)	4 (4)	5 (5)	6 (6)	7 (7)	8 (8)	9 (0)
10 (1)	11 (2)	12 (3)	13 (4)	14 (5)	15 (6)	16 (7)	17 (8)	18 (0)
19 (1)	20 (2)	21 (3)	22 (4)	23 (5)	24 (6)	25 (7)	26 (8)	27 (0)
28 (1)	29 (2)	30 (3)	31 (4)	32 (5)	33 (6)	34 (7)	35 (8)	36 (0)
37 (1)	38 (2)	39 (3)	40 (4)	41 (5)	42 (6)	43 (7)	44 (8)	45 (0)
46 (1)	47 (2)	48 (3)	49 (4)	50 (5)	51 (6)	52 (7)	53 (8)	54 (0)
55 (1)	56 (2)	57 (3)	58 (4)	59 (5)	60 (6)	61 (7)	62 (8)	63 (0)
64 (1)	65 (2)	66 (3)	67 (4)	68 (5)	69 (6)	70 (7)	71 (8)	72 (0)
73 (1)	74 (2)	75 (3)	76 (4)	77 (5)	78 (6)	79 (7)	80 (8)	81 (0)
82 (1)	83 (2)	84 (3)	85 (4)	86 (5)	87 (6)	88 (7)	89 (8)	90 (0)
91 (1)	92 (2)	93 (3)	94 (4)	95 (5)	96 (6)	97 (7)	98 (8)	99 (0)
100 (1)	101 (2)	102 (3)	103 (4)	104 (5)	105 (6)	106 (7)	107 (8)	108 (0)

For addition, the check numbers of each number must equal the check number of the sum. For subtraction, the remainder plus the number being subtracted must equal the number you started with.

Use check numbers to find the wrong answers. Correct the wrong answers. Put check marks by the ones that agree with the check numbers. The first one is done.

```
   39 (3)        28          75          24          65          83          38
 + 21 (3)      + 57        + 29        + 47        + 29        + 31        + 39
   60 (6)✓      75         105          72          94         124          79


   52           71          34         106          38          82         103
 - 13         - 48        - 29        - 87        - 19        - 45        - 94
   39           37           5          21          27          47           9
```

D: © Joan A. Cotter 2001

Worksheet 40-A, Review

Name _____

Date _____

1. Write only the answers to the oral questions. _____ _____ _____

4. Write only the answers. 64 − 56 = _____   72 − 23 = _____   95 − 43 = _____

7. Write the multiples of 4.

___ ___ ___ ___ ___

___ ___ ___ ___ ___

17. 4 × 6 = ____   4 × 2 = ____

19. 4 × 3 = ____   4 × 5 = ____

21. 4 × 4 = ____   4 × 10 = ____

23. 4 × 1 = ____   4 × 8 = ____

25. 4 × 9 = ____   4 × 7 = ____

27. This is 1 triangle. Draw $1\frac{1}{2}$ triangles.

28. Find the missing numbers.

```
   _____       _____
 − 6578      − 5476
  ─────      ─────
   2349       2954
```

29. Use digits and write this number in the proper order: 2 hundred, 8 ones, and 7 thousand.

_____

30. Jamie is buying four small gifts for $1.26 each. What is the total cost?

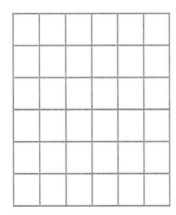

31. A library has 5 thousand 6 hundred 6 books. Of these 1368 books are checked out. How many books does the library have in?

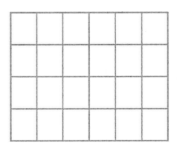

D: © Joan A. Cotter 2001

Worksheet 40-B, Review

Name _____

Date _____

1. Write only the answers to the oral questions. _____ _____ _____

4. Write only the answers. 82 – 27 = _____   98 – 50 = _____   98 – 55 = _____

7. Write the multiples of 9.

____ ____ ____ ____ ____

____ ____ ____ ____ ____

17. 9 × 5 = ____   9 × 8 = ____

19. 9 × 7 = ____   9 × 9 = ____

21. 9 × 1 = ____   9 × 4 = ____

23. 9 × 6 = ____   9 × 3 = ____

25. 9 × 2 = ____   9 × 10 = ____

27. This is 1 triangle. Draw $2\frac{1}{2}$ triangles.

28. Find the missing numbers.

```
  _____        _____
– 4 6 5 4    – 5 7 9 3
  3 1 9 7      3 6 8 4
```

29. Use digits and write this number in the proper order: 7 tens, 9 hundred, 8 thousand.

_____

30. Morgan is buying five small gifts for $2.38 each. What will they cost?

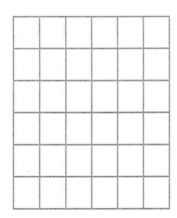

31. Six thousand eighty-one children live in the town of Rockville. Of these 3086 are girls. How many are boys?

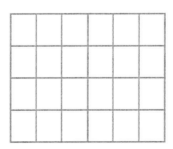

D: © Joan A. Cotter 2001

Worksheet 41, Finding Check Numbers

Name _____

Date _____

Find the check numbers for these numbers. Each check number will be different.

4214( )   6936( )   7892( )   4968( )

2588( )   5674( )   3895( )   6375( )

Add the following numbers. Use check numbers to check your work.

```
  7832        8863        5737        5326
+ 1446       + 687       + 2546      + 1788
```

```
  4136        2557         972        4145
   120        3271        1785         819
+ 5186      + 2582      + 8557      + 2733
```

Subtract the following numbers. Use check numbers to check your work.

```
  3641        6565        5232        7900
- 1262       - 3542      - 5053      - 5073
```

```
  5586        3628        8405        5067
- 2689       - 2811      - 1687      - 3368
```

Worksheet 42, The "Almost" Subtraction Strategy

Name _____

Date _____

Solve these problems in your head. Explain how you found the answers.

1. A customer bought a bag of groceries for $3.01 and pays for it with $5. How much change does the customer get back?

2. Mindy is buying some rolls that cost $2.99. She pays for it with a five dollar bill. How much money does she get back?

3. A video program is 1 hour and 58 minutes long. If it is started at 7:00, what time will it be over?

4. Matt's brother is reading a thick book with 200 pages. He has two pages left to read. What page is he on?

Subtract these in your head. Think of the *almost* strategy. Use check numbers for the third row.

14	11	13	16	14	12	17	13	15
−5	−2	−5	−7	−8	−3	−9	−4	−6

23	38	65	72	53	97	34	46	80
−4	−9	−7	−3	−5	−8	−6	−7	−1

425	187	247	105	636	300	312
−26	−88	−49	−7	−37	−1	−13

D: © Joan A. Cotter 2001

Worksheet 43, Terry's Way to Subtract

Name _____

Date _____

Terry found another way to subtract. Terry's friends like it because they don't need to use any facts like 11 – 6. Here are some examples. What do you think?

```
   54        852       6592
  -29       -375      -4284
   30        500       2000
   -5        -20        300
   25         -3         10
             477         -2
                       2308
```

Before you say, "I don't get it," let Terry explain it to you.

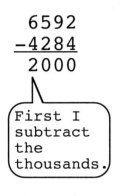
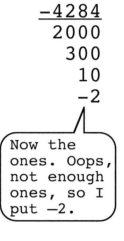
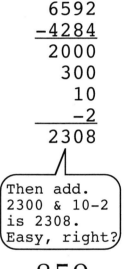

Now you try it. Be sure to check your work.

```
  76    77    51    62    64    610    859
 -13   -69    -9   -35   -48   -112   -375
```

```
  792    821   6076   3843   7083   6005
 -139   -626  -4753  -3346  -2249  -1009
```

One more thing: Terry wants to know what we should call this method.

_____

D: © Joan A. Cotter 2001

Worksheet 44, Working With Twos

Name _____

Date _____

Write these when your teacher says start. Time _____ Number right _____

2	2	2	2	2	2	2	2	2	2
x4	x9	x7	x3	x8	x1	x2	x10	x5	x6

Write addition and multiplication equations for each array.

$2 \times 3 = $ ____

_____

$2 \times 6 = $ ____

_____

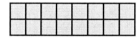

$2 \times 1 = $ ____

_____

$2 \times 8 = $ ____

_____

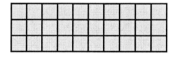

$2 \times 10 = $ ____

_____

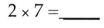

$2 \times 7 = $ ____

_____

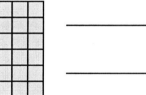

$2 \times 5 = $ ____

_____

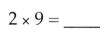

$2 \times 9 = $ ____

_____

$2 \times 4 = $ ____

_____

$2 \times 2 = $ ____

Write these when your teacher says start. Time _____ Number right _____

10	4	9	6	7	5	1	3	2	8
x2	x2	x2	x2	x2	x2	x2	x2	x2	x2

D: © Joan A. Cotter 2001

Worksheet 45-A, Review

Name _____

Date _____

1. Write only the answers to the oral questions. _____ _____ _____

4. Write only the answers: 67 − 28 = _____   43 − 29 = _____   62 − 18 = _____

7. Write the multiples of 3.

____ ____ ____

____ ____ ____

____ ____ ____

____

17.
3 × 1 = ___   3 × 2 = ___   3 × 3 = ___

3 × 4 = ___   3 × 5 = ___   3 × 6 = ___

3 × 7 = ___   3 × 8 = ___   3 × 9 = ___

3 × 10 = ___

27. Write the check numbers.

14 ____   99 ____

457 ____   852 ____

31. Jamie is buying three notebooks for $2.58 each. What is the total cost?

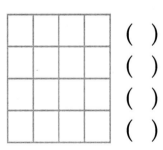
( )
( )
( )
( )

32. A pair of boots costs $19.85. A coat costs $35.37 and a cap costs $7.47. What is the total cost?

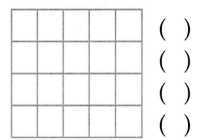
( )
( )
( )
( )

33. 569   34. 756   35. 7823   36. 1365
   − 284   − 157   − 4905   − 846

37. 2 × 5 = ___   2 × 8 = ___   2 × 4 = ___   2 × 9 = ___   2 × 6 = ___

D: © Joan A. Cotter 2001

Worksheet 45-B, Review

Name _____

Date _____

1. Write only the answers to the oral questions. _____ _____ _____

4. Write only the answers: 54 − 35 = _____   100 − 29 = _____   88 − 37 = _____

7. Write the multiples of 4.

____ ____ ____ ____ ____

____ ____ ____ ____ ____

17. 4 × 8 = ____   4 × 4 = ____

19. 4 × 3 = ____   4 × 5 = ____

41. 4 × 4 = ____   4 × 10 = ____

43. 4 × 1 = ____   4 × 6 = ____

45. 4 × 7 = ____   4 × 9 = ____

27. Write the check numbers.

25 ____   63 ____   178 ____   467 ____

31. Jamie is buying three notebooks for 4 dollars and 9 cents each. What is the total cost?

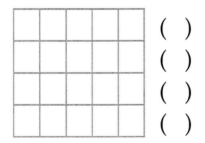

( )
( )
( )
( )

32. A pair of gloves costs $4.27. A scarf costs $8.99 and a hat costs $13.59. What is the total cost?

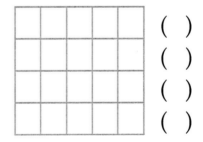

( )
( )
( )
( )

33. 346
   − 271

34. 532
   − 133

35. 6539
   − 2632

36. 2864
   − 975

37. 3 × 1 = ____   3 × 10 = ____   3 × 2 = ____   3 × 5 = ____   3 × 3 = ____

D: © Joan A. Cotter 2001

Worksheet 46, Working With Fives

Name _____

Date _____

Write these when your teach says start. Time _____   Number right _____

5	5	5	5	5	5	5	5	5	5
×3	×10	×6	×5	×9	×8	×1	×2	×7	×4

Time _____

Number right _____

5 × 3 = ____

5 × 6 = ____

5 × 1 = ____

5 × 8 = ____

5 × 10 = ____

5 × 7 = ____

5 × 5 = ____

5 × 9 = ____

5 × 4 = ____

5 × 2 = ____

Draw arrows pointing to the numbers.

1. 4, 19, 23

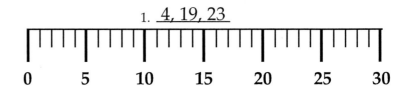

2. 12, 1, 26

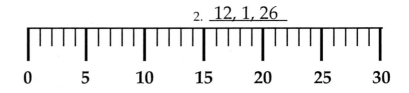

Write the numbers that the arrows are pointing to.

3. _____

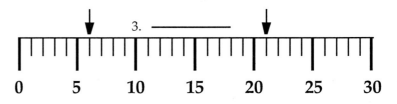

4. _____

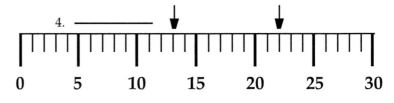

5. _____

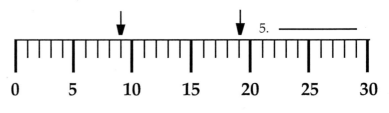

6. _____

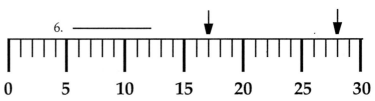

D: © Joan A. Cotter 6.1.2005

Worksheet 47, Quick Practice-1

Name _____

Date _____

Date _____ Time _____ Number right _____

2	2	2	2	2	2	2	2	2	2
×7	×2	×9	×6	×4	×1	×10	×3	×5	×8

5	5	5	5	5	5	5	5	5	5
×6	×5	×3	×1	×10	×4	×9	×8	×7	×2

Date _____ Time _____ Number right _____

4	10	3	6	5	8	1	7	9	2
×2	×2	×2	×2	×2	×2	×2	×2	×2	×2

5	2	6	4	3	10	1	7	9	8
×5	×5	×5	×5	×5	×5	×5	×5	×5	×5

Date _____ Time _____ Number right _____

5	2	2	3	2	8	10	2	2	2
×2	×6	×4	×2	×2	×2	×2	×7	×9	×1

5	2	9	5	6	5	5	5	4	5
×7	×5	×5	×3	×5	×8	×10	×5	×5	×1

Date _____ Time _____ Number right _____

5	5	5	2	4	2	6	2	5	5
×9	×8	×2	×7	×10	×5	×5	×1	×3	×2

1	1	10	1	10	10	10	1	1	10
×9	×5	×4	×3	×10	×8	×2	×1	×6	×7

D: © Joan A. Cotter 2001

Worksheet 48, Telling Time to the Minute

Name _____

Date _____

Draw the hands for each clock.

9:35   9:36   9:38   9:34

12:11   3:47   5:58   1:23

11:17   8:08   10:29   7:51

Write the time for each clock.

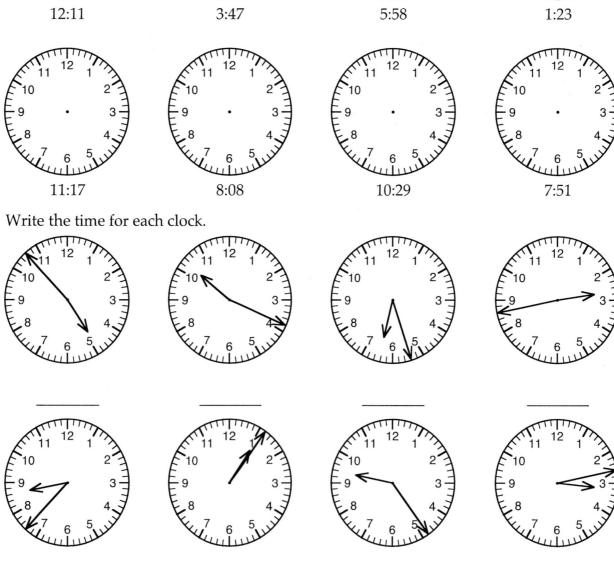

_____   _____   _____   _____

_____   _____   _____   _____

D: © Joan A. Cotter 2001

Worksheet 49, Multiplying With Money

Name _____

Date _____

Write the multiplication equations.

b. _____

c. _____

a. _____

Draw pictures to show the following equations. Use a circle with *N* to show a nickel, a circle with *D* to show a dime, and a circle with *Q* to show a quarter. Complete the equations.

(N) (D) (Q)

d. 5¢ × 8 = _____   e. 10¢ × 6 = _____   f. 25¢ × 4 = _____

D: © Joan A. Cotter 2001

Worksheet 50, Multiplying With 1s and 0s

Name _____

Date _____

Write the multiplication equations.

a. _____   b. _____   c. _____

Draw the pictures to show the following equations. Which is more? _____

d. 5¢ × 1 = _____   e. 1¢ × 5 = _____

```
  3      1      1      5      2      1      8      6      1      7
 ×1     ×9     ×5     ×1     ×1     ×7     ×1     ×1     ×1     ×1


  1      9      1      4      1      1      1     10      1      1
 ×6     ×1     ×1     ×1    ×10     ×0     ×4     ×1     ×8     ×3


  9     10      3      0      0      0      6      1      0      0
 ×0     ×0     ×0     ×0     ×5     ×3     ×0     ×0     ×4     ×6


  8      7      0      0      2      0      5      4      0      0
 ×0     ×0     ×9     ×7     ×0     ×1     ×0     ×0    ×10     ×8
```

How much is zero times any number? Explain.

D: © Joan A. Cotter 2001

Worksheet 51-A, Review

Name _____

Date _____

1. Write only the answers to the oral questions. _____ _____ _____

4. Write only the answers. 64 – 47 = _____   72 – 23 = _____   95 + 47 = _____

7. Write the multiples of 6.

17. 3691
   – 2837

18. 3082
   – 984

___ ___ ___ ___ ___

___ ___ ___ ___ ___

19. Draw the hands for these two clocks.

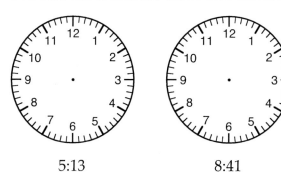

5:13   8:41

21. Write the time on these two clocks.

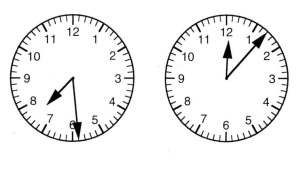

_____   _____

23. Explain how you can tell how many squares there are without counting each one.

24. How many trees are still growing in North Park? They planted 54 walnut trees, 638 oak trees and 89 maple trees. But storms killed 10 trees.

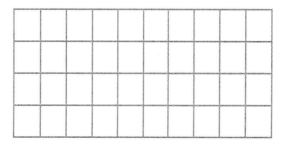

26.   7   10   2   4   5   9   0   1
    ×5   ×2   ×8   ×10   ×8   ×5   ×212   ×486

D: © Joan A. Cotter 2001

Worksheet 51-B, Review

Name _____

Date _____

1. Write only the answers to the oral questions. _____ _____ _____

4. Write only the answers. 82 − 29 = _____   94 − 46 = _____   96 + 57 = _____

7. Write the multiples of 8.

17. 6431
   − 4916

18. 9550
   − 955

___ ___ ___ ___ ___

___ ___ ___ ___ ___

19. Draw the hands for these two clocks.

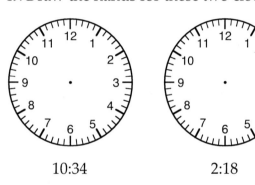

10:34   2:18

21. Write the time on these two clocks.

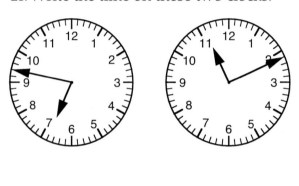

_____   _____

23. Explain how you can tell how many squares there are without having to count each one.

24. Lauren had 10 dollars and bought some food for $3.28 and a ticket for a ride for $2.75. How much money does Lauren have left?

26.   9   4   2   4   5   7   578   267
     ×5   ×2   ×7   ×5   ×6   ×5   ×0   ×1

D: © Joan A. Cotter 2001

Worksheet 52, Quick Practice-2

Name _____

Date _____ Time _____ Number right _____/50

1 × 1 = ____	2 × 9 = ____	5 × 5 = ____	3 × 5 = ____	8 × 1 = ____
2 × 8 = ____	6 × 2 = ____	2 × 7 = ____	2 × 4 = ____	9 × 5 = ____
2 × 1 = ____	1 × 5 = ____	8 × 0 = ____	5 × 3 = ____	6 × 5 = ____
5 × 8 = ____	9 × 2 = ____	3 × 2 = ____	7 × 1 = ____	4 × 2 = ____
2 × 6 = ____	7 × 5 = ____	5 × 10 = ____	8 × 2 = ____	9 × 1 = ____
5 × 2 = ____	10 × 5 = ____	5 × 7 = ____	1 × 3 = ____	5 × 4 = ____
6 × 1 = ____	10 × 1 = ____	8 × 5 = ____	2 × 2 = ____	10 × 2 = ____
1 × 8 = ____	7 × 2 = ____	2 × 5 = ____	5 × 1 = ____	5 × 6 = ____
0 × 5 = ____	2 × 10 = ____	1 × 7 = ____	5 × 9 = ____	3 × 1 = ____
4 × 5 = ____	2 × 3 = ____	6 × 0 = ____	1 × 4 = ____	1 × 9 = ____

Date _____ Time _____ Number right _____/50

9 × 5 = ____	2 × 3 = ____	8 × 1 = ____	1 × 4 = ____	2 × 7 = ____
5 × 9 = ____	8 × 2 = ____	1 × 7 = ____	0 × 5 = ____	9 × 2 = ____
2 × 4 = ____	5 × 5 = ____	2 × 8 = ____	4 × 5 = ____	5 × 10 = ____
8 × 5 = ____	5 × 3 = ____	5 × 1 = ____	9 × 1 = ____	2 × 10 = ____
5 × 8 = ____	5 × 7 = ____	10 × 5 = ____	4 × 2 = ____	2 × 6 = ____
6 × 0 = ____	3 × 1 = ____	5 × 2 = ____	2 × 1 = ____	3 × 2 = ____
1 × 1 = ____	1 × 8 = ____	7 × 5 = ____	8 × 0 = ____	1 × 5 = ____
6 × 2 = ____	1 × 9 = ____	3 × 5 = ____	10 × 1 = ____	2 × 2 = ____
5 × 4 = ____	5 × 6 = ____	2 × 5 = ____	6 × 1 = ____	1 × 3 = ____
7 × 1 = ____	10 × 2 = ____	6 × 5 = ____	2 × 9 = ____	7 × 2 = ____

D: © Joan A. Cotter 2001

Worksheet 53, Multiplication Problems

Name _____

Date _____

Explain your work and write equations.

1. Megan practiced handwriting for 10 minutes every day last week. How much time was that?

2. Matt and his brothers have 9 pairs of shoes altogether. How many shoes is that?

3. Mario set the table for 8 people. He set 1 knife, 2 forks, and 2 spoons at each place. How many utensils did he set?

4. Marva wants to buy a notebook for 50¢. She has 9 nickels. Is that enough money?

5. Mike earns two dollars a day for delivering papers. How much money does he make in a week?

6. Madison saved $1 every day in March. How much did she save during the month?

7. Maria bought four books at four dollar each. She also bought zero books at three dollars each. How much did she pay?

8. Mark bought 2 dozen eggs. How many eggs is that?

D: © Joan A. Cotter 2001

Worksheet 54, Multiplication Table

Name _____

Date _____

Multiplication Table

×	1	2	3	4	5	6	7	8	9	10
1										
2										
3										
4										
5										
6										
7										
8										
9										
10										

Write the multiples of 4.

Write the multiples of 3.

____ ____ ____ ____ ____   ____ ____ ____

____ ____ ____ ____ ____   ____ ____ ____

Write the multiples of 6.   ____

____ ____ ____ ____ ____

____ ____ ____ ____ ____

D: © Joan A. Cotter 2001

Worksheet 55, Quick Practice-3

Name _____

Date _____ Time _____ Number right ____/40

10	2	8	8	1	2	5	5	7	2
×2	×7	×5	×2	×2	×5	×5	×8	×5	×6

10	9	3	2	5	2	1	5	2	2
×5	×5	×2	×10	×3	×9	×10	×10	×0	×8

2	0	5	4	1	2	6	5	4	10
×3	×5	×1	×5	×1	×2	×5	×7	×2	×7

6	3	5	2	2	5	9	5	5	7
×2	×5	×4	×4	×1	×6	×2	×9	×2	×2

Date _____ Time _____ Number right ____/50

4	2	3	5	8	5	6	3	2	10
×3	×6	×8	×10	×3	×7	×3	×6	×8	×3

8	6	7	5	5	5	6	1	2	10
×5	×2	×2	×1	×2	×6	×5	×2	×9	×7

5	8	4	3	7	3	2	1	9	3
×3	×2	×5	×7	×5	×4	×5	×3	×3	×1

9	9	5	7	3	10	5	2	2	5
×2	×5	×8	×3	×10	×2	×5	×2	×3	×9

3	4	2	5	5	3	1	3	3	10
×5	×2	×7	×2	×4	×3	×5	×9	×2	×5

D: © Joan A. Cotter 2001

Worksheet 56, Working With Threes

Name _____

Date _____

3	3	3	3	3	3	3	3	3	3
×9	×7	×2	×3	×1	×8	×10	×5	×6	×4

3	1	8	6	2	5	4	7	10	9
×3	×3	×3	×3	×3	×3	×3	×3	×3	×3

3 × 4 = _____   8 × 3 = _____   How many days are in 3 weeks? _____

3 × 2 = _____   6 × 3 = _____   How many minutes are in 3 hours? _____

3 × 1 = _____   5 × 3 = _____

3 × 10 = _____   2 × 3 = _____   1 quart has 32 ounces.
                                    How many ounces are in 3 quarts? _____

3 × 6 = _____   3 × 3 = _____

3 × 3 = _____   10 × 3 = _____

                                    How many hours are in 3 days? _____

3 × 8 = _____   1 × 3 = _____

3 × 5 = _____   7 × 3 = _____

3 × 9 = _____   4 × 3 = _____   How many days are in 3 years? _____

3 × 7 = _____   9 × 3 = _____

D: © Joan A. Cotter 2001

Worksheet 57, Quick Practice-4

Name _____

| Date _____ | Time _____ | Number right _____ /50 |

1	7	10	10	7	2	5	8	5	3
×5	×5	×2	×5	×2	×5	×1	×3	×7	×3

4	3	6	4	5	10	8	5	3	5
×2	×7	×3	×3	×3	×7	×5	×2	×5	×2

3	1	2	5	8	6	2	10	3	2
×1	×3	×7	×5	×2	×5	×6	×3	×4	×2

5	4	3	3	5	3	2	5	7	9
×10	×5	×8	×6	×4	×2	×9	×6	×3	×2

2	5	2	5	1	6	3	3	9	9
×3	×8	×8	×9	×2	×2	×9	×10	×3	×5

| Date _____ | Time _____ | Number right _____ /50 |

3	5	5	4	3	3	2	5	3	6
×2	×6	×2	×3	×4	×6	×5	×4	×5	×2

10	5	7	10	5	6	5	10	5	2
×5	×5	×2	×3	×1	×5	×7	×2	×10	×7

9	10	8	4	1	4	2	2	3	6
×3	×7	×5	×2	×3	×5	×9	×6	×9	×3

9	9	3	1	2	8	7	2	8	5
×2	×5	×3	×2	×2	×3	×5	×3	×2	×2

3	5	1	3	7	3	2	3	5	5
×8	×8	×5	×7	×3	×1	×8	×10	×3	×9

D: © Joan A. Cotter 2001

Worksheet 58, Reviewing Place Value

Name _____

Date _____

Each cube represents 1. Write the quantity below the figure.

a.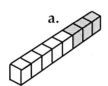

b.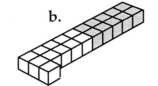

c.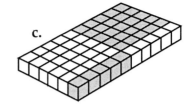

_____   _____   _____

d. e.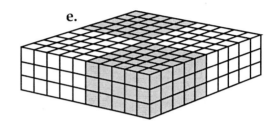

_____   _____

f. g.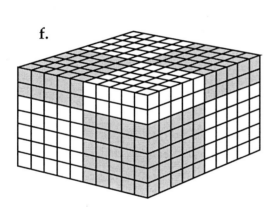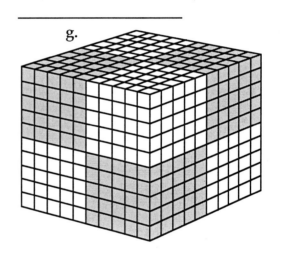

_____   _____

Find the sums.

a+b	a+c	c+d
a+d	b+d	c+c
e+a	d+e	e+b
d+f	e+c	e+f
e+f+a	e+f+g	a+b+c+d+e+f+g

D: © Joan A. Cotter 2001

Worksheet 59-A, Review

Name _____

Date _____

1. Write only the answers to the oral questions. _____ _____ _____

4. Write only the answers. 64 – 47 = _____   72 – 48 = _____   95 + 93 = _____

7. Write the multiples of 8.

___ ___ ___ ___ ___

___ ___ ___ ___ ___

17. Kim has three bags. Each has nine books. How many books does Kim have? Write the equation.

_____

19. Draw the hands for these two clocks.

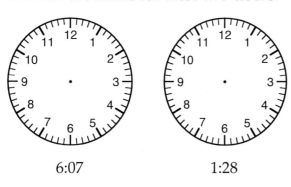

6:07   1:28

21. Write the time on these two clocks.

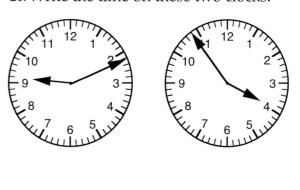

_____   _____

23. Each square is a box with 2 mittens. How many mittens are there altogether? Write the equation.

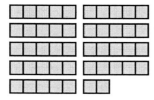

24. A 4-H club is planting 300 trees. On Monday they planted 57 trees. On Tuesday they planted 116 trees. How many trees do they have left to plant?

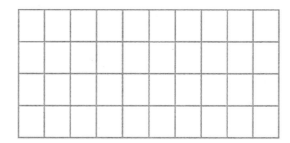

26.   3   189   428   9   5   3   3   8
     ×5   ×1   ×0   ×5   ×8   ×6   ×7   ×3

D: © Joan A. Cotter 2001

Worksheet 59-B, Review

Name _____

Date _____

1. Write only the answers to the oral questions. _____ _____ _____

4. Write only the answers. 82 – 54 = _____   43 – 29 = _____   94 + 98 = _____

7. Write the multiples of 9.

___ ___ ___ ___ ___

___ ___ ___ ___ ___

17. Kerry has three packages. Each has 100 cards. How many cards does Kerry have altogether? Write the equation.

_____

19. Draw the hands for these two clocks.

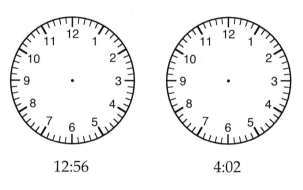

12:56   4:02

21. Write the time on these two clocks.

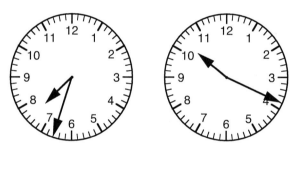

_____   _____

23. Each square is a box with 2 shoes. How many shoes are there altogether? Write the equation.

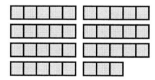

24. A group of scouts is trying to raise $100. They made $36.49 on Friday and $52.86 on Saturday. How much do they have left to raise?

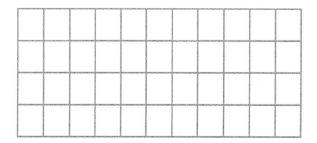

26.   3   1   3   0   3   5   5   3
    × 6   × 76   × 5   × 3   × 8   × 6   × 7   × 3

D: © Joan A. Cotter 2001

Worksheet 60, Working With Fours

Name _____

Date _____

4	4	4	4	4	4	4	4	4	4
x6	x10	x5	x2	x8	x9	x4	x1	x7	x3

7	2	5	6	8	1	10	4	9	3
x4	x4	x4	x4	x4	x4	x4	x4	x4	x4

4 × 4 = _____   2 × 4 = _____

4 × 1 = _____   5 × 4 = _____

4 × 7 = _____   1 × 4 = _____

4 × 5 = _____   4 × 4 = _____

4 × 10 = _____   10 × 4 = _____

4 × 8 = _____   7 × 4 = _____

4 × 6 = _____   3 × 4 = _____

4 × 3 = _____   6 × 4 = _____

4 × 9 = _____   9 × 4 = _____

4 × 2 = _____   5 × 4 = _____

4 × 5 = _____   8 × 4 = _____

1. How many days are in 4 weeks? _____
Is that more or less than a month?

2. How many minutes are in 4 hours? _____

3. 1 foot has 12 inches.
How many inches are in 4 feet? _____

4. A pizza shop owner cuts pizzas into fourths.
How many slices can she get from 5 pizzas?

5. How many hours are in 4 days? _____

D: © Joan A. Cotter 2001

Worksheet 61, Quick Practice-5

Name _____

Date _____ Time _____ Number right _____/50

5	4	3	5	8	4	2	3	4	8
×4	×8	×3	×9	×3	×4	×3	×2	×9	×5

1	6	9	7	4	9	2	5	5	6
×3	×2	×2	×3	×3	×5	×8	×3	×7	×4

2	2	3	9	3	9	4	4	6	5
×7	×6	×9	×4	×8	×3	×5	×2	×3	×5

4	2	8	5	8	5	3	3	4	7
×1	×9	×2	×6	×7	×5	×5	×6	×7	×2

4	0	2	3	6	7	5	5	8	2
×6	×5	×4	×4	×5	×4	×2	×8	×4	×5

Date _____ Time _____ Number right _____/50

1	5	8	6	9	3	3	4	4	9
×3	×5	×3	×3	×4	×3	×8	×1	×4	×2

7	8	2	5	2	4	9	3	5	6
×2	×5	×3	×6	×9	×7	×0	×9	×9	×4

2	7	3	4	9	3	2	8	6	2
×5	×5	×5	×3	×5	×6	×6	×4	×2	×8

9	4	4	2	4	2	5	4	5	4
×3	×2	×9	×4	×4	×2	×2	×8	×8	×6

5	5	4	7	7	2	3	6	3	8
×7	×3	×5	×4	×3	×7	×4	×5	×7	×2

D: © Joan A. Cotter 2001

Worksheet 62, Representing Many Thousands

Name _____

Date _____

Each cube represents 1000. Write the quantity below the figure.

a. 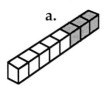   b. 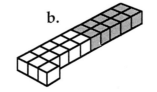   c.

_____   _____   _____

d. 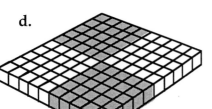   e.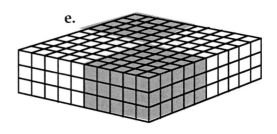

f. 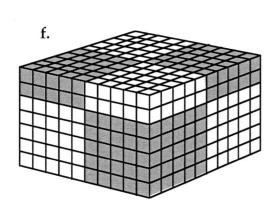   g.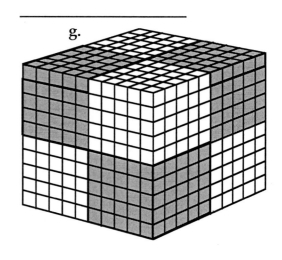

_____   _____

_____   _____

Find the sums.

a+b	a+c	c+d
a+d	b+d	c+c
e+a	d+e	e+b
d+f	e+c	e+f
e+f+a	e+f+g	a+b+c+d+e+f+g

D: © Joan A. Cotter 2001

Worksheet 63, Building Thousands

Name _____

Date _____

Each cube represents 1000. Write the quantity below the figure.

a.

b.

c.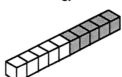

d.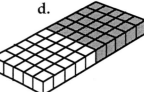

_____ _____   _____   _____

e.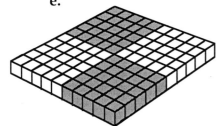

f.

_____   _____

Find the figures needed to construct the numbers in the first column. Write the number of figures needed in the correct columns. No number may be > 4.

		f.	e.	d.	c.	b.	a.
g.	8,000					1	3
h.	36 thousand						
i.	three hundred one thousand						
j.	nine hundred ten thousand						
k.	1 million						
l.	six hundred sixty-six thousand						
m.	217,000						
n.	480 thousand						
o.	one million five thousand						

D: © Joan A. Cotter 2001

Worksheet 64-1, Digits and Commas

Cut apart on the solid lines. Make large numbers as your teacher directs.

1	2	3	4
5	6	7	8
9	0	0	0
,	,	0	0

D: © Joan A. Cotter 2001

Worksheet 64-2, Reading and Writing Large Numbers

Name _____

Date _____

Write these as numbers.

a. 10 thousand _____   b. 72 thousand _____

c. 102 thousand _____   d. 245 thousand _____

e. 950 thousand _____   f. 1 million _____

g. 8 million _____   h. 12 million _____

Write the number on the line. The answers are in the boxes.
Cross them out as you use them.

i. 6 hundred 20 thousand 6 hundred two _____

j. 62 thousand 62 _____

k. 6 thousand 2 hundred sixty-two _____

l. 602 thousand 6 hundred twenty-two _____

m. six hundred twenty-two thousand sixty-two _____

n. 622 thousand 6 hundred two _____

6,262
62,062
622,062
622,602
620,602
602,622

Write these number in words.

o. 41,632 _____

_____

p. 519,803 _____

_____

q. 303,073 _____

_____

D: © Joan A. Cotter 2001

Worksheet 65, Quick Practice-6

Name _____

Date _____ Time _____ Number right _____/50

4	3	4	7	1	5	6	4	5	3
×6	×3	×9	×3	×3	×2	×5	×7	×8	×5

3	7	3	8	2	7	4	3	8	2
×6	×4	×9	×5	×4	×5	×4	×2	×3	×6

4	2	5	6	2	9	4	8	2	5
×5	×9	×6	×3	×8	×4	×2	×4	×7	×7

3	4	6	5	6	5	4	9	3	5
×0	×1	×2	×4	×2	×9	×3	×3	×4	×5

6	5	3	7	9	9	2	3	4	2
×4	×3	×8	×2	×5	×2	×5	×7	×8	×3

Date _____ Time _____ Number right _____/50

5	4	4	8	9	2	3	3	5	1
×6	×8	×2	×2	×3	×3	×2	×9	×9	×3

3	9	5	2	4	5	2	7	5	5
×4	×4	×3	×6	×5	×2	×4	×2	×0	×4

9	4	2	9	5	6	7	5	2	6
×2	×3	×5	×5	×7	×4	×3	×5	×9	×3

4	4	3	5	3	5	3	2	3	2
×6	×1	×5	×8	×7	×4	×3	×7	×8	×8

8	7	4	6	3	3	4	8	8	6
×3	×5	×4	×2	×7	×6	×9	×5	×4	×5

D: © Joan A. Cotter 2001

Worksheet 66, Working With Large Numbers

Name _____

Date _____

a. The earth is not perfectly round. It is 24,902 miles around at the equator and 24,860 miles around the poles. How much farther is it around at the equator?

b. If a hole could be bored through the earth at the equator, it would be 95,112 feet long. If it were bored at the poles, it would be 94,788 feet. What is the difference between the two distances?

c. The closest the moon is from the earth is 221,456 miles; the farthest is 252,711 miles? What is the difference between the closest and farthest distances?

d. The distance around the moon is 6,790 miles. The distance around the earth is 24,902 miles. How much less is the distance around the moon?

e. Light travels very fast. It travels 186,282 miles in 1 second. How far does it travel in 2 seconds? Could light reach the moon in 2 seconds?

f. How far does light travel in 4 seconds?

g. There are 5,280 feet in a mile. What is the perimeter of the park in feet. The park has a square shape as shown in the figure.

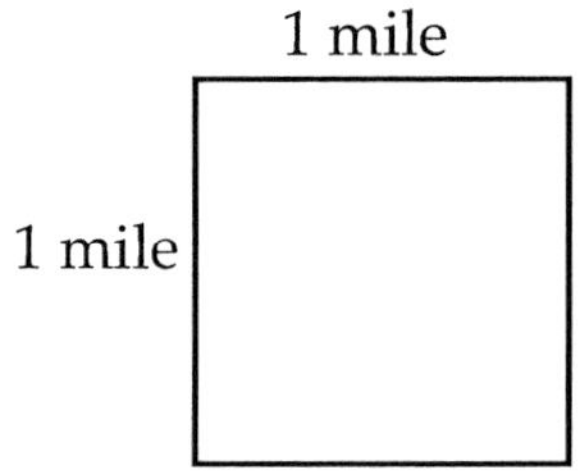

1 mile

1 mile

D: © Joan A. Cotter 2001

Worksheet 67, Working With Nines

Name _____

Date _____

9	9	9	9	9	9	9	9	9	9
×3	×9	×6	×5	×1	×10	×8	×4	×2	×7

2	10	7	6	5	1	8	4	3	9
×9	×9	×9	×9	×9	×9	×9	×9	×9	×9

9 × 8 = ____   5 × 9 = ____   a. How many days are in 9 weeks? ____
                                  Is that more or less than 2 months?

9 × 2 = ____   2 × 9 = ____

9 × 1 = ____   10 × 9 = ____   b. How many minutes are in 9 hours? ____

9 × 6 = ____   9 × 9 = ____

9 × 10 = ____   3 × 9 = ____   c. 1 quart has 32 ounces.
                                  How many ounces are in 9 quarts?

9 × 9 = ____   6 × 9 = ____

9 × 5 = ____   8 × 9 = ____

9 × 7 = ____   4 × 9 = ____   d. Baseball teams need 9 players.
                                  How many players are needed for 8 teams?

9 × 3 = ____   1 × 9 = ____

9 × 4 = ____   7 × 9 = ____   e. How many days are in 9 years? ____

D: © Joan A. Cotter 2001

Worksheet 68-A, Review

Name _____

Date _____

1. Write only the answers to the oral questions. _____ _____ _____

4. Write only the answers. 76 + 47 = _____ 64 − 48 = _____ 92 − 89 = _____

7. Write the multiples of 9.

17.
9 × 8 = ____   6 × 9 = ____

9 × 4 = ____   7 × 9 = ____

9 × 1 = ____   3 × 9 = ____

____ ____ ____ ____ ____

____ ____ ____ ____ ____

23. Explain how you could find 9 × 6 if you didn't know it.

_____

24. The population of Indiana is 6,080,000. Write this number in words.

_____

25. In City Bank, there are 28 bags with money. Each bag has 1 thousand dollars. How much money is in the bags?

_____

26. A machine is packing seeds by putting one thousand seeds in a bag. How many bags will the machine fill for 17,000 seeds?

_____

27. Three million four hundred eighty-five thousand three hundred ninety-eight people live in Los Angeles. Write this number using digits.

_____

28. In 1990, the population of Saint Paul was 272,235. The population of Minneapolis was 368,383. How many people lived in those 2 cities that year?

29.
```
  808,791      560,567
+ 352,240    − 63,945
```

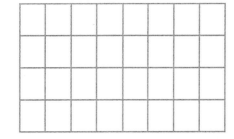

Worksheet 68-B, Review

Name _____

Date _____

1. Write only the answers to the oral questions. _____ _____ _____

4. Write only the answers. 55 + 88 = _____   75 − 39 = _____   81 − 76 = _____

7. Write the multiples of 4.

17.
$4 \times 7 =$ ____ $9 \times 4 =$ ____

$4 \times 5 =$ ____ $6 \times 4 =$ ____

____ ____ ____ ____ ____

$4 \times 8 =$ ____ $4 \times 4 =$ ____

____ ____ ____ ____ ____

23. Explain how you could find 4×9 if you didn't know it.

_____

24. The population of Colorado is 4,300,000. Write this number in words.

_____

25. State Bank has $49,000 in bags. Each bag has one thousand dollars. How many bags do they have?

_____

26. A seed corn dealer has 83 bags of seed. Each bag has about 1000 seeds. About how many seeds is that all together?

_____

27. One million six hundred thirty thousand five hundred fifty-three people live in Houston. Write this number using digits.

_____

28. In 1990, the population of Dallas was 1,006,877. The population of Fort Worth was 447,619. How many people lived in those 2 cities that year?

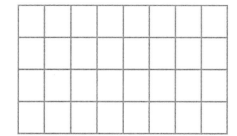

29.
622,199
+ 414,249

875,208
− 35,487

Worksheet 69, Quick Practice-7

Name _____

Date _____	Time _____	Number right _____/50		
3 × 4 = ____	7 × 4 = ____	4 × 9 = ____	6 × 9 = ____	9 × 2 = ____
8 × 9 = ____	9 × 9 = ____	3 × 2 = ____	3 × 5 = ____	2 × 3 = ____
5 × 9 = ____	9 × 8 = ____	4 × 6 = ____	9 × 3 = ____	5 × 4 = ____
3 × 3 = ____	3 × 8 = ____	6 × 5 = ____	0 × 9 = ____	9 × 6 = ____
4 × 8 = ____	9 × 4 = ____	6 × 3 = ____	6 × 2 = ____	4 × 4 = ____
7 × 9 = ____	4 × 2 = ____	3 × 6 = ____	2 × 8 = ____	2 × 9 = ____
3 × 7 = ____	1 × 9 = ____	3 × 9 = ____	2 × 4 = ____	7 × 3 = ____
6 × 4 = ____	4 × 5 = ____	9 × 5 = ____	5 × 7 = ____	9 × 10 = ____
2 × 6 = ____	8 × 3 = ____	4 × 7 = ____	8 × 5 = ____	9 × 7 = ____
4 × 3 = ____	9 × 1 = ____	5 × 6 = ____	8 × 4 = ____	5 × 3 = ____

Date _____	Time _____	Number right _____/50		
3 × 9 = ____	4 × 4 = ____	6 × 2 = ____	3 × 4 = ____	8 × 9 = ____
3 × 2 = ____	3 × 8 = ____	5 × 4 = ____	4 × 3 = ____	3 × 6 = ____
9 × 9 = ____	3 × 7 = ____	0 × 9 = ____	5 × 3 = ____	6 × 4 = ____
9 × 8 = ____	6 × 9 = ____	9 × 3 = ____	1 × 9 = ____	4 × 2 = ____
9 × 2 = ____	9 × 10 = ____	5 × 6 = ____	8 × 5 = ____	4 × 9 = ____
2 × 3 = ____	9 × 5 = ____	3 × 3 = ____	5 × 9 = ____	6 × 3 = ____
2 × 4 = ____	6 × 5 = ____	4 × 8 = ____	9 × 4 = ____	9 × 7 = ____
4 × 5 = ____	2 × 8 = ____	8 × 3 = ____	2 × 6 = ____	3 × 5 = ____
7 × 3 = ____	7 × 9 = ____	7 × 4 = ____	9 × 6 = ____	5 × 7 = ____
4 × 6 = ____	2 × 9 = ____	4 × 7 = ____	8 × 4 = ____	9 × 1 = ____

D: © Joan A. Cotter 2001

Worksheet 70, Multiplying and Adding

Name _____

Date _____

Write the equations to show the number of squares, using multiplication and addition.

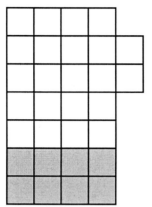

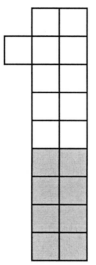

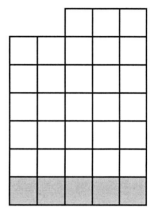

a. _____

c. _____

b. _____

Use multiplication and addition to find the sums.

d. 325
325
325
325
325
325
325
+325

e. 3,025
3,025
3,025
3,025
+3,025

f. 879
879
879
+879

g. 52,078
+52,078

h. 91,463
91,463
91,463
+91,463

i. 2,468
2,468
2,468
2,468
2,468
2,468
2,468
2,468
2,468
+2,468

Write problems e, f, and i as multiplication problems.

D: © Joan A. Cotter 2001

Worksheet 71, Multiplying by a 1-Digit Number

Name _____

Date _____

Multiply.

1.
$$\begin{array}{r} 32 \\ \times\ 3 \\ \hline \end{array}$$
$$\begin{array}{r} 21 \\ \times\ 4 \\ \hline \end{array}$$
$$\begin{array}{r} 44 \\ \times\ 5 \\ \hline \end{array}$$

4.
$$\begin{array}{r} 25 \\ \times\ 5 \\ \hline \end{array}$$
$$\begin{array}{r} 813 \\ \times\ 3 \\ \hline \end{array}$$
$$\begin{array}{r} 439 \\ \times\ 2 \\ \hline \end{array}$$

7.
$$\begin{array}{r} 235 \\ \times\ 4 \\ \hline \end{array}$$
$$\begin{array}{r} 160 \\ \times\ 5 \\ \hline \end{array}$$
$$\begin{array}{r} 322 \\ \times\ 3 \\ \hline \end{array}$$

10.
$$\begin{array}{r} 858 \\ \times\ 3 \\ \hline \end{array}$$
$$\begin{array}{r} 2{,}719 \\ \times\ 4 \\ \hline \end{array}$$
$$\begin{array}{r} 829 \\ \times\ 5 \\ \hline \end{array}$$

13.
$$\begin{array}{r} 7{,}519 \\ \times\ 3 \\ \hline \end{array}$$
$$\begin{array}{r} 1{,}211 \\ \times\ 9 \\ \hline \end{array}$$
$$\begin{array}{r} 6{,}084 \\ \times\ 5 \\ \hline \end{array}$$

16.
$$\begin{array}{r} 9{,}005 \\ \times\ 2 \\ \hline \end{array}$$
$$\begin{array}{r} 2{,}520 \\ \times\ 6 \\ \hline \end{array}$$
$$\begin{array}{r} 8619 \\ \times\ 9 \\ \hline \end{array}$$

D: © Joan A. Cotter 2001

Worksheet 72, Quick Practice--8

Name _____

Date _____ Time _____ Number right _____ /50

2	7	6	2	2	8	3	4	9	8
×6	×4	×5	×8	×9	×9	×5	×4	×0	×5

4	3	3	1	6	9	3	5	8	5
×2	×6	×7	×9	×4	×2	×4	×4	×3	×6

7	7	4	9	3	3	2	3	8	9
×2	×3	×9	×8	×3	×2	×4	×8	×4	×1

3	4	5	8	6	4	4	9	6	9
×9	×7	×9	×2	×3	×8	×3	×5	×9	×7

4	4	9	5	9	9	7	9	5	6
×6	×5	×4	×3	×9	×3	×9	×6	×7	×2

Date _____ Time _____ Number right _____ /50

2	8	4	5	5	9	3	8	3	4
×9	×4	×3	×9	×4	×0	×2	×3	×6	×5

6	9	7	9	4	5	8	4	9	6
×9	×7	×3	×5	×4	×3	×2	×2	×8	×5

4	7	3	3	6	8	9	3	1	8
×6	×2	×4	×5	×3	×9	×1	×8	×9	×5

6	3	9	9	6	4	9	2	3	3
×2	×3	×2	×4	×4	×7	×6	×4	×9	×7

4	7	2	7	5	9	5	2	9	4
×9	×4	×6	×9	×7	×9	×6	×8	×3	×8

D: © Joan A. Cotter 2001

Worksheet 73, Introducing Area

Name _____

Date _____

Write the measurements of the rectangles in inches. Find the perimeters and the areas.

1.

2.

3.

D: © Joan A. Cotter 2001

Worksheet 74, Working With Square Inches

Name _____

Date _____

Write the measurements of the rectangles in inches. Find the areas in square inches.

1.

2.

3.

D: © Joan A. Cotter 2001

Worksheet 75, Quick Practice--9   Name _____

Date _____   Time _____   Number right _____ /50

9	6	3	8	2	5	9	9	4	3
×7	×9	×6	×9	×4	×6	×0	×3	×7	×8

4	7	9	4	4	6	4	5	3	6
×6	×9	×8	×9	×2	×4	×5	×9	×9	×3

7	8	2	3	9	5	6	4	9	3
×4	×5	×8	×5	×5	×3	×2	×3	×9	×2

4	9	3	1	9	5	3	9	5	6
×4	×2	×7	×9	×6	×7	×3	×1	×4	×5

7	9	2	3	4	8	7	2	8	8
×3	×4	×9	×4	×8	×3	×2	×6	×4	×2

Date _____   Time _____   Number right _____ /50

9	1	8	4	7	3	4	6	3	2
×2	×9	×3	×9	×4	×5	×3	×2	×3	×9

8	3	4	3	4	3	8	6	2	7
×4	×6	×4	×9	×2	×8	×2	×4	×4	×9

9	2	3	2	6	9	5	9	5	3
×5	×8	×4	×6	×3	×0	×7	×3	×9	×2

9	5	4	6	9	5	9	3	9	7
×9	×4	×6	×9	×8	×6	×4	×7	×1	×3

4	4	9	8	5	7	9	8	6	4
×8	×5	×7	×5	×3	×2	×6	×9	×5	×7

D: © Joan A. Cotter 2001

Worksheet 76, Working With Sixes

Name _____

Date _____

6	6	6	6	6	6	6	6	6	6
×3	×4	×1	×7	×9	×5	×8	×6	×2	×10

2	5	7	8	3	10	6	1	4	9
×6	×6	×6	×6	×6	×6	×6	×6	×6	×6

6 × 10 = ____   7 × 6 = ____

a. How many days are in 6 weeks? _____
Is that more or less than 2 months?

6 × 2 = ____   10 × 6 = ____

6 × 5 = ____   8 × 6 = ____

b. North Bank handles 8 million dollars a day. How much is that in a week from Monday to Saturday?

6 × 6 = ____   3 × 6 = ____

6 × 4 = ____   9 × 6 = ____

c. 1 quart has 32 ounces.
How many ounces are in 6 quarts?

6 × 1 = ____   5 × 6 = ____

6 × 3 = ____   2 × 6 = ____

6 × 7 = ____   4 × 6 = ____

d. Hockey teams need 6 players.
How many players are needed for 8 teams?

6 × 8 = ____   1 × 6 = ____

6 × 9 = ____   6 × 6 = ____

e. How many days are in 6 years? _____

D: © Joan A. Cotter 2001

Worksheet 77-A, Review

Name _____

Date _____

1. Write only the answers to the oral questions. _____ _____ _____

4. Write only the answers. 2000 × 7 = _____   156 – 49 = _____   99 + 89 = _____

7. This line is an inch long. Draw a square inch. _____

8. A class spends 55 minutes every day in math class. How much time is that in a week (5 days)?

9. What is the area of the figure below in square inches?

10. The population of North Dakota is 642,000. Write this number in words.

_____

_____

11. The population of Wyoming is four hundred ninety-three thousand seven hundred eighty-two. Write this number in digits.

_____

12. Martin Luther King, Jr. was born in 1929 and died in 1968. How old was he when he died? Explain.

13. A certain new car costs twenty-four thousand six hundred eighteen dollars. What do two new cars cost?

D: © Joan A. Cotter 2001

Worksheet 77-B, Review

Name _____

Date _____

1. Write only the answers to the oral questions. _____ _____ _____

4. Write only the answers. 2000 × 9 = _____   163 – 56 = _____   99 + 72 = _____

7. This line is an inch long. Draw a square inch.

8. A grade class spends 65 minutes every day at lunch and recess. How much time is that in a week (5 days)?

9. What is the area of the figure below in square inches?

10. The population of Alaska is 627,000. Write this number in words.

_____

_____

11. The population of Vermont is six hundred eight thousand eight hundred twenty-seven. Write this number in digits.

_____

12. John F. Kennedy was born in 1917 and died in 1963. How long did he live?

13. A certain new boat costs fifteen thousand seven hundred sixty-one dollars. What do 3 new boats cost?

D: © Joan A. Cotter 2001

Worksheet 78-1, Working With Centimeters

Name _____

Date _____

1. Draw a line 6 centimeters long.

2. Draw a line $4\frac{1}{2}$ centimeters long.

3. Draw 1 square centimeter.

4. Draw 3 square centimeters.

Write the measurements for the following rectangles in centimeters. How many square centimeters fill the rectangles? Write the area in sq cm.

5.

6.

7.

8.

D: © Joan A. Cotter 2001

Worksheet 78-2, Working With Centimeters

Name _____

Date _____

Measure the following rectangles in centimeters. Then find the area in sq cm.

1.

2.

3.

4.

5.

D: © Joan A. Cotter 2001

Worksheet 79, Quick Practice-10

Name _____

Date _____ Time _____ Number right _____ /50

9	4	5	9	4	3	7	7	2	5
×5	×7	×4	×1	×3	×8	×2	×3	×4	×3

8	3	3	4	1	4	3	9	3	3
×9	×9	×4	×5	×9	×4	×6	×7	×5	×2

6	3	8	9	5	9	7	2	8	4
×5	×3	×4	×8	×6	×6	×4	×9	×2	×8

2	6	9	5	2	8	5	6	9	6
×8	×9	×4	×9	×6	×5	×7	×2	×9	×4

6	4	7	9	9	4	6	8	3	4
×0	×6	×9	×2	×3	×2	×3	×3	×7	×9

Date _____ Time _____ Number right _____ /50

5	3	8	4	3	2	7	4	1	2
×4	×9	×5	×3	×3	×9	×4	×6	×9	×8

6	9	5	9	8	3	6	7	3	4
×9	×3	×6	×2	×9	×5	×4	×3	×2	×7

3	5	2	9	6	2	9	3	8	9
×8	×9	×4	×0	×5	×6	×1	×7	×2	×6

9	8	6	8	4	4	7	4	9	7
×4	×3	×2	×4	×9	×5	×9	×4	×9	×2

6	9	5	4	3	5	4	9	3	9
×3	×8	×3	×2	×4	×7	×8	×7	×6	×5

D: © Joan A. Cotter 2001

Worksheet 80-1, Finding Areas

Name _____

Partner _____

Date _____

Find the area of the figure below in square units. Each little square is a square unit. Color the areas different colors. Solve the problem in two ways.

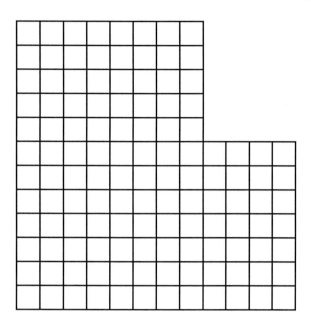

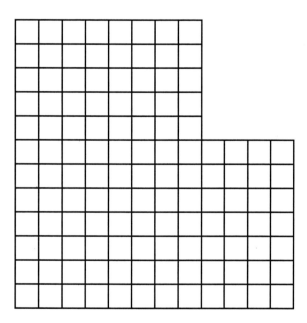

D: © Joan A. Cotter 2001

Worksheet 80-2, Finding Areas

Name _____

Date _____

Find the area of the following figure two different ways.

1.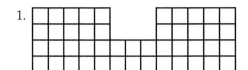

2.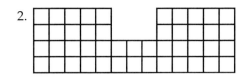

Find the area in square units.

3.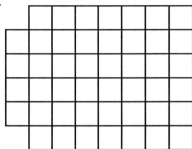

4.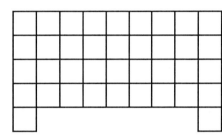

5.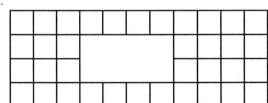

6.

D: © Joan A. Cotter 2001

Worksheet 81, Area Problems

Name _____

Date _____

1. The Lee family is laying a patio with patio stones that are 1 foot square. How many patio stones do they need? See the figure at the right.

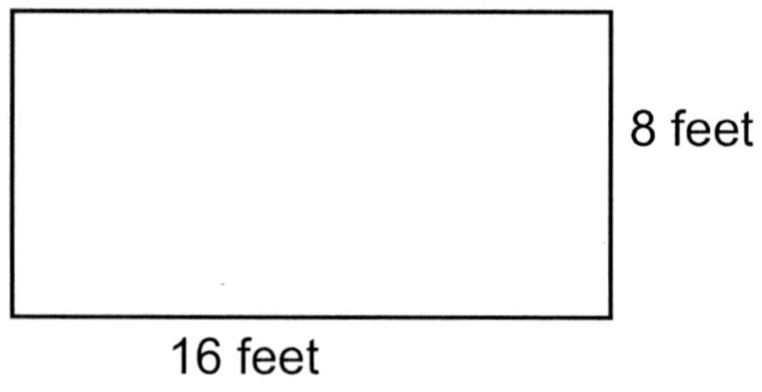

8 feet

16 feet

The patio measurements.

2. What will the patio stones cost? They are paying six dollars for each patio stone.

3. Next the Lee family decides to build a fence around the patio. How many feet of fencing do they need?

4. Fencing costs $10 a foot. What is the cost of the fence?

5. What is the total cost of the patio, the stones and the fence?

6. How many square feet are in the auditorium shown in the figure?

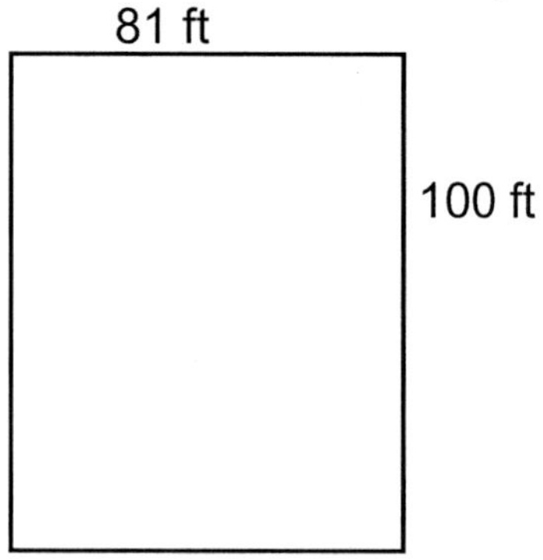

81 ft

100 ft

7. How many square inches are in the rectangle shown in the figure?

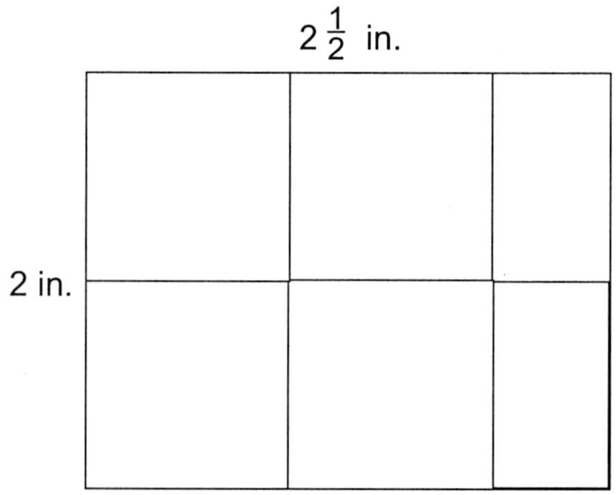

$2\frac{1}{2}$ in.

2 in.

D: © Joan A. Cotter 2001

Worksheet 82, Quick Practice-11   Name _____

Date _____ Time _____ Number right _____/50

8 × 3 = ____	6 × 9 = ____	2 × 8 = ____	9 × 5 = ____	5 × 3 = ____
4 × 5 = ____	5 × 6 = ____	4 × 6 = ____	7 × 9 = ____	6 × 5 = ____
4 × 9 = ____	5 × 4 = ____	1 × 9 = ____	5 × 7 = ____	3 × 3 = ____
7 × 4 = ____	6 × 4 = ____	9 × 3 = ____	3 × 2 = ____	5 × 9 = ____
2 × 4 = ____	9 × 1 = ____	3 × 7 = ____	9 × 4 = ____	8 × 2 = ____
9 × 6 = ____	8 × 4 = ____	9 × 8 = ____	7 × 2 = ____	3 × 4 = ____
9 × 7 = ____	3 × 6 = ____	4 × 2 = ____	8 × 9 = ____	3 × 8 = ____
4 × 4 = ____	6 × 2 = ____	4 × 7 = ____	2 × 6 = ____	3 × 5 = ____
8 × 5 = ____	9 × 2 = ____	7 × 3 = ____	3 × 9 = ____	9 × 9 = ____
6 × 3 = ____	4 × 8 = ____	9 × 0 = ____	2 × 9 = ____	4 × 3 = ____

Date _____ Time _____ Number right _____/50

8 × 8 = ____	4 × 6 = ____	9 × 8 = ____	6 × 9 = ____	5 × 7 = ____
8 × 6 = ____	4 × 9 = ____	3 × 5 = ____	5 × 8 = ____	3 × 6 = ____
8 × 0 = ____	6 × 5 = ____	8 × 4 = ____	4 × 5 = ____	2 × 7 = ____
1 × 8 = ____	8 × 9 = ____	5 × 6 = ____	3 × 7 = ____	8 × 3 = ____
3 × 9 = ____	7 × 9 = ____	4 × 8 = ____	8 × 2 = ____	5 × 4 = ____
9 × 7 = ____	7 × 6 = ____	6 × 3 = ____	7 × 8 = ____	6 × 6 = ____
3 × 8 = ____	4 × 4 = ____	9 × 9 = ____	8 × 7 = ____	9 × 4 = ____
8 × 1 = ____	2 × 8 = ____	5 × 9 = ____	8 × 5 = ____	7 × 3 = ____
9 × 3 = ____	7 × 4 = ____	9 × 5 = ____	6 × 8 = ____	4 × 3 = ____
4 × 7 = ____	6 × 4 = ____	9 × 6 = ____	2 × 9 = ____	3 × 4 = ____

D: © Joan A. Cotter 2001

Worksheet 83, Working With Eights

Name _____

Date _____

8	8	8	8	8	8	8	8	8	8
×6	×2	×8	×3	×5	×7	×9	×1	×4	×10

2	10	8	6	7	9	4	1	3	5
×8	×8	×8	×8	×8	×8	×8	×8	×8	×8

8 × 5 = ____   2 × 8 = ____

a. A spider has 8 legs. Each leg has 7 knees. How many knees does a spider have?

8 × 10 = ____   5 × 8 = ____

8 × 8 = ____   6 × 8 = ____

b. A ticket to a concert costs $8 plus a $1 handling charge for each ticket. How much will 8 tickets cost?

8 × 1 = ____   8 × 8 = ____

8 × 6 = ____   7 × 8 = ____

c. During the month of April, a nurse sleeps 8 hours every night. How many hours did the nurse spend sleeping.

8 × 3 = ____   9 × 8 = ____

8 × 7 = ____   4 × 8 = ____

d. The cubs ordered 7 pizzas. Each one was cut into 8 pieces. How many pieces are there in all?

8 × 9 = ____   10 × 8 = ____

8 × 2 = ____   1 × 8 = ____

e. Baseball teams need 9 players. How many players are needed for 8 teams?

8 × 4 = ____   3 × 8 = ____

f. How many months are in 8 years? _____

D: © Joan A. Cotter 2001

Worksheet 84, Multiplying Three Numbers

Name _____

Date _____

Find the products.

5 × 2 × 4 = ____   4 × 5 × 3 = ____   2 × 3 × 6 = ____   3 × 2 × 10 = ____

4 × 2 × 5 = ____   4 × 3 × 5 = ____   6 × 3 × 2 = ____   10 × 2 × 3 = ____

5 × 4 × 2 = ____   5 × 3 × 4 = ____   2 × 6 × 3 = ____   3 × 10 × 2 = ____

Find the products. If you need space for your work, use the area below.

2 × 10 × 5 = _____   5 × 8 × 1 = _____   7 × 10 × 0 = _____

5 × 17 × 2 = _____   20 × 3 × 3 = _____   2 × 8 × 5 = _____

15 × 7 × 2 = _____   12 × 4 × 10 = _____   13 × 10 × 2 _____

6 × 25 × 4 = _____   20 × 7 × 5 = _____   6 × 10 × 8 = _____

3 × 20 × 3 = _____   100 × 0 × 6 = _____   7 × 6 × 100 = _____

Multiply.

```
    68           17          215           32
  × 20         × 50         × 30         × 40
  ____         ____         ____         ____
```

```
    32          156          948          795
  × 40         × 30         × 70         × 80
  ____         ____         ____         ____
```

D: © Joan A. Cotter 2001

Worksheet 85-A, Review

Name _____

Date _____

1. Write only the answers to the oral questions. _____ _____ _____

4. Write only the answers. $2 \times 7 \times 5 =$ _____ $60 - 31 =$ _____ $101 + 67 =$ _____

7. Which rectangle below has the greater area? Explain your work.

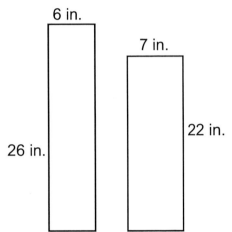

11. Which rectangle has the greater perimeter? Show your work.

13. What is the area of the room below in square feet?

12 ft
9 ft

15. How many tiles are needed to cover the floor? Each tile is 1 square foot. What is the cost? Each tile costs $6.

17.
```
  8,579      5,031      5,829       573
+19,334    - 4,056       × 8       × 50
```

Worksheet 85-B, Review

Name _____

Date _____

1. Write only the answers to the oral questions. _____ _____ _____

4. Write only the answers. $8 \times 2 \times 5 =$ _____ $80 - 19 =$ _____ $106 + 43 =$ _____

7. Which rectangle below has the greater area? Explain your work.

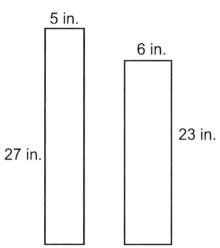

11. Which rectangle has the greater perimeter? Show your work.

13. What is the area of the room below in square feet?

15. How many tiles are needed to cover the floor? Each tile is 1 square foot. What is the cost? Each tile costs $9.

17.
$$\begin{array}{r} 9{,}832 \\ +33{,}872 \end{array} \qquad \begin{array}{r} 3{,}119 \\ -2{,}123 \end{array} \qquad \begin{array}{r} 2{,}487 \\ \times \ 6 \end{array} \qquad \begin{array}{r} 709 \\ \times \ 80 \end{array}$$

Worksheet 86, Quick Practice-12

Name _____

| Date _____ | Time _____ | Number right ____ /50 |

3	8	5	9	6	9	8	1	9	9
×6	×5	×9	×7	×4	×8	×4	×8	×9	×5

4	6	8	2	6	8	9	6	4	4
×8	×6	×1	×8	×9	×2	×4	×5	×3	×5

7	3	9	8	5	8	3	8	8	3
×9	×8	×3	×9	×7	×0	×9	×7	×3	×7

4	6	7	2	7	5	6	7	8	3
×6	×8	×8	×7	×4	×8	×3	×3	×6	×4

2	5	3	5	8	7	4	9	4	4
×9	×4	×5	×6	×8	×6	×4	×6	×7	×9

| Date _____ | Time _____ | Number right ____ /50 |

1	8	5	4	2	2	9	8	5	6
×8	×6	×8	×6	×7	×9	×3	×4	×6	×9

3	5	8	4	4	7	9	8	3	9
×4	×7	×9	×3	×8	×9	×8	×3	×9	×4

6	4	9	8	5	3	7	6	4	2
×5	×7	×6	×0	×4	×7	×6	×3	×9	×8

8	7	8	7	3	3	8	7	9	6
×8	×4	×1	×8	×6	×5	×7	×3	×5	×4

5	4	9	8	9	6	4	3	8	6
×9	×5	×7	×2	×9	×6	×4	×8	×5	×8

D: © Joan A. Cotter 2001

Worksheet 87, Arrays of Cubes

Name _____

Date _____

Find the number of cubes in each array. Write the equations.

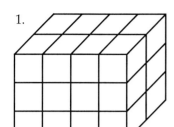
1.

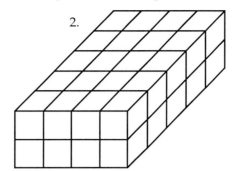
2.

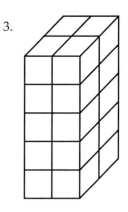
3.

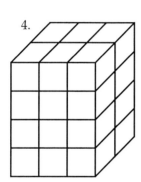
4.

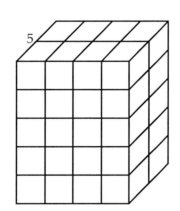
5.

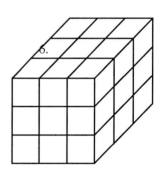
6.

Draw freehand arrays with the dimensions given below. Some lines are drawn for you.

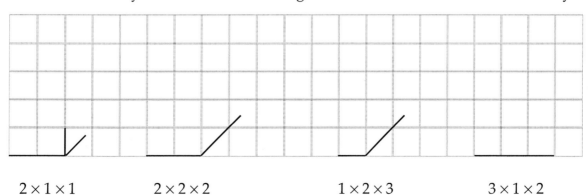

$2 \times 1 \times 1$ $2 \times 2 \times 2$ $1 \times 2 \times 3$ $3 \times 1 \times 2$

D: © Joan A. Cotter 2001

Worksheet 88, Working With Sevens

Name _____

Date _____

7	7	7	7	7	7	7	7	7	7
×4	×3	×7	×9	×1	×6	×2	×5	×8	×10

7	10	3	6	5	9	1	4	8	2
×7	×7	×7	×7	×7	×7	×7	×7	×7	×7

7 × 10 = ____   2 × 7 = ____   a. How many days are in six weeks?

7 × 7 = ____   9 × 7 = ____

7 × 9 = ____   5 × 7 = ____   b. A person is buying 7 tickets. Each ticket costs $7. How much change will there be from a $100 bill?

7 × 1 = ____   10 × 7 = ____

7 × 2 = ____   1 × 7 = ____

                                  c. A foot is 12 inches. How many inches tall is a person who is 7 feet tall?

7 × 4 = ____   6 × 7 = ____

7 × 5 = ____   7 × 7 = ____

7 × 3 = ____   3 × 7 = ____

                                  d. How many minutes are in 7 hours?

7 × 6 = ____   4 × 7 = ____

7 × 8 = ____   8 × 7 = ____

                                  e. How many hours are in a week? ____

D: © Joan A. Cotter 2001

Worksheet 89, Quick Practice-13

Name _____

Date _____ Time _____ Number right _____ /50

9	7	5	6	4	7	5	6	8	8
×7	×4	×7	×5	×7	×3	×4	×8	×9	×5

9	7	5	4	9	6	9	4	6	2
×3	×8	×6	×3	×6	×6	×8	×4	×7	×7

7	4	7	6	7	8	4	0	9	5
×5	×8	×9	×4	×6	×7	×6	×7	×5	×8

3	4	5	8	1	3	7	8	7	2
×7	×5	×5	×4	×7	×8	×7	×8	×1	×9

9	7	6	3	2	9	8	4	5	3
×9	×2	×9	×9	×8	×4	×6	×9	×9	×6

Date _____ Time _____ Number right _____ /50

9	9	7	2	4	9	4	3	9	5
×6	×3	×6	×8	×7	×5	×4	×8	×7	×7

4	7	4	6	4	5	3	1	8	6
×9	×5	×6	×8	×5	×6	×6	×7	×6	×4

4	8	9	7	8	5	2	5	7	7
×3	×8	×9	×7	×4	×4	×9	×8	×2	×4

5	0	8	7	3	4	6	9	6	3
×9	×7	×5	×8	×9	×8	×6	×8	×7	×7

6	2	9	8	6	7	5	7	8	7
×9	×7	×4	×9	×5	×9	×5	×1	×7	×3

D: © Joan A. Cotter 2001

Worksheet 90, Seeing Patterns

Name _____

Date _____

Draw terms 4 and 5.
Complete the table.

Term	1	2	3	4	5	10	20
Number of squares	4	8	___	___	___	___	___

Explain how the pattern grows and how you found the answers for the table.

Draw terms 4 and 5.
Complete the table.

Term	1	2	3	4	5	___	___
Number of squares	1	4	___	___	___	81	100

Explain how the pattern grows and how you found the answers for the table.

D: © Joan A. Cotter 2001

Worksheet 91, Patterns With Squares

Name _____

Date _____

Draw the fourth and fifth terms and complete the table.

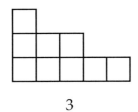

1

2

3

4

5

Term	1	2	3	4	5	6	7
Number of squares	1	___	___	___	___	___	___

Draw the fourth and fifth terms and complete the table.

1   2   3   4   5

Term	1	2	3	4	5	6	7
Number of circles	___	___	___	___	___	___	___

Use your calculator and circle the numbers that are perfect squares.

   1   81   48   100   64   90   900   10,000   4900   15

   5   49   35   144   25   15   200   25,000   2500   25

D: © Joan A. Cotter 2001

Worksheet 92, Quick Practice--14

Name _____

```
Date _____   Time _____   Number right _____ /50

  6     7     8     4     8     9     4     8     5     6
 ×9    ×7    ×9    ×6    ×6    ×5    ×7    ×8    ×9    ×6

  3     6     7     3     6     9     7     9     7     8
 ×4    ×5    ×6    ×3    ×8    ×3    ×9    ×8    ×4    ×3

  9     6     5     9     4     9     8     4     3     8
 ×2    ×4    ×3    ×4    ×5    ×9    ×5    ×8    ×9    ×4

  5     6     3     5     3     7     5     3     8     3
 ×8    ×3    ×7    ×4    ×5    ×3    ×7    ×6    ×7    ×8

  4     9     5     7     6     7     9     4     5     4
 ×9    ×6    ×6    ×5    ×7    ×8    ×7    ×3    ×5    ×4

Date _____   Time _____   Number right _____ /50

  8     4     8     6     3     8     7     6     4     7
 ×9    ×6    ×8    ×9    ×4    ×3    ×7    ×8    ×7    ×9

  6     9     4     7     5     7     9     5     3     8
 ×3    ×6    ×5    ×8    ×7    ×6    ×3    ×4    ×8    ×4

  3     9     5     4     7     4     6     6     5     4
 ×5    ×4    ×6    ×3    ×4    ×8    ×6    ×7    ×3    ×9

  9     4     7     5     7     3     9     8     8     5
 ×5    ×4    ×3    ×8    ×5    ×3    ×2    ×6    ×7    ×5

  3     9     8     3     5     9     3     6     9     6
 ×6    ×7    ×5    ×7    ×9    ×8    ×9    ×5    ×9    ×4
```

D: © Joan A. Cotter 2001

Worksheet 93, A Squares Pattern

Name _____

Date _____

When a number is multiplied by itself, it is often written with a little 2 written higher. For example, 5 × 5 is written 5^2 and is equal to 25. Read it as 5 squared.

Find the following numbers squared.

5^2 = __25__ 4^2 = _____ 2^2 = _____

1^2 = _____ 8^2 = _____ 10^2 = _____

3^2 = _____ 9^2 = _____ 7^2 = _____

6^2 = _____ 0^2 = _____ 8^2 = _____

In the second row, write the product of 1 more and 1 less than the squared number.

3 × 3 = _____	9 × 9 = _____
4 × 2 = _____	__ × __ = _____
4 × 4 = _____	8 × 8 = _____
__ × __ = _____	__ × __ = _____

Write the squares from 2^2 to 9^2 in the table. Write the product of 1 more and 1 less than the square. (5^2 is done.)

×	1	2	3	4	5	6	7	8	9	10
1										
2										
3										
4					24					
5				25						
6				24						
7										
8										
9										
10										

Use your calculator to square the number. Use the pattern to find the other product.

17 × 17 = _____	15 × 15 = _____	11 × 11 = _____	13 × 13 = _____
18 × 16 = _____	16 × 14 = _____	12 × 10 = _____	14 × 12 = _____
20 × 20 = _____	29 × 29 = _____	30 × 30 = _____	40 × 40 = _____
21 × 19 = _____	30 × 28 = _____	31 × 29 = _____	41 × 39 = _____

D: © Joan A. Cotter 2001

Worksheet 94-A, Review

Name _____

Date _____

1. Write only the answers to the oral questions. _____ _____ _____

4. Write only the answers. 9^2 = _____   200 − 41 = _____   146 + 39 = _____

7. Find the number of cubes in the array. Write the equation.

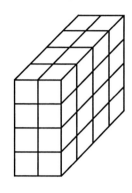

8. Use a pattern to find the products.

7 × 7 = _____

8 × 6 = _____

27 × 27 = 729

28 × 26 = _____

9. Draw the fourth term and complete the table.

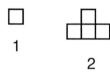

1   2   3   4

Term	1	2	3	4	5	6	10
Number of squares	1	4	___	___	___	___	___

16. How many hours are in a week?

17. Jamie has 9 quarters, 8 dimes, and 12 pennies. How much money is that?

19.

```
  3,916        4,000        4,157         623
  3,682      − 2,098        ×    7       ×  20
+ 3,405
```

D: © Joan A. Cotter 2001

Worksheet 94-B, Review

Name _____

Date _____

1. Write only the answers to the oral questions. _____ _____ _____

4. Write only the answers. 8^2 = _____   200 − 29 = _____   153 + 28 = _____

7. Find the number of cubes in the array. Write the equation.

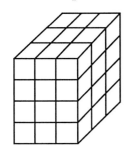

8. Use a pattern to find the products.

$7 \times 7 =$ _____

$6 \times 8 =$ _____

$28 \times 28 = 784$

$29 \times 27 =$ _____

9. Draw the fourth term and complete the table.

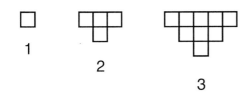

1   2   3   4

Term	1	2	3	4	5	6	10
Number of squares	1	4	___	___	___	___	___

16. How many minutes are in a day?

17. Jordan has 7 quarters, 9 dimes, and 13 pennies. How much money is that?

19.

```
  5,829        6,000       6,482         752
  6,868      − 3,076        × 7         × 20
+ 5,309
```

D: © Joan A. Cotter 2001

Worksheet 95, Continuing the Pattern

Name _____

Date _____

Write the next terms in the patterns. For numbers 14 and 15, make up your own pattern. Then ask another person to continue the pattern.

1.   3   6   9   12   _____   _____

2.   2   4   8   16   _____   _____

3.   1   4   9   16   _____   _____

4.   6   11   16   21   _____   _____

5.   1   3   6   10   _____   _____

6.   11   22   33   44   _____   _____

7.   20   19   18   17   _____   _____

8.   25   50   75   100   _____   _____

9.   2   12   22   32   _____   _____

10.   1   10   100   1,000   _____   _____

11. $\frac{1}{2}$ 1 $1\frac{1}{2}$ 2   _____   _____

12.   16   8   4   2   _____   _____

13. $\frac{1}{2}$ $1\frac{1}{2}$ $2\frac{1}{2}$ $3\frac{1}{2}$ _____   _____

14.   _____   _____   _____   _____   _____   _____

15.   _____   _____   _____   _____   _____   _____

D: © Joan A. Cotter 2001

Worksheet 96, Quick Practice-15

Name _____

Date _____ Time _____ Number right _____/50

5 × 6 = ____	4 × 4 = ____	9 × 7 = ____	6 × 9 = ____	7 × 4 = ____
9 × 2 = ____	6 × 5 = ____	3 × 8 = ____	5 × 7 = ____	5 × 3 = ____
4 × 5 = ____	9 × 4 = ____	3 × 7 = ____	7 × 5 = ____	8 × 8 = ____
3 × 6 = ____	6 × 4 = ____	4 × 9 = ____	5 × 5 = ____	8 × 6 = ____
5 × 4 = ____	4 × 8 = ____	9 × 3 = ____	5 × 9 = ____	8 × 5 = ____
8 × 7 = ____	6 × 3 = ____	9 × 6 = ____	8 × 4 = ____	3 × 9 = ____
4 × 3 = ____	7 × 7 = ____	3 × 3 = ____	6 × 7 = ____	7 × 9 = ____
8 × 3 = ____	9 × 9 = ____	3 × 4 = ____	8 × 9 = ____	6 × 8 = ____
4 × 6 = ____	3 × 5 = ____	7 × 8 = ____	4 × 7 = ____	5 × 8 = ____
9 × 5 = ____	7 × 3 = ____	6 × 6 = ____	9 × 8 = ____	7 × 6 = ____

Date _____ Time _____ Number right _____/50

5 × 5 = ____	9 × 6 = ____	7 × 4 = ____	9 × 8 = ____	5 × 4 = ____
4 × 7 = ____	7 × 8 = ____	8 × 3 = ____	6 × 8 = ____	5 × 3 = ____
7 × 7 = ____	6 × 7 = ____	3 × 4 = ____	8 × 7 = ____	3 × 9 = ____
9 × 4 = ____	3 × 5 = ____	9 × 7 = ____	8 × 5 = ____	9 × 3 = ____
4 × 4 = ____	6 × 3 = ____	5 × 8 = ____	7 × 5 = ____	5 × 6 = ____
9 × 9 = ____	6 × 6 = ____	4 × 5 = ____	5 × 7 = ____	3 × 8 = ____
9 × 5 = ____	8 × 6 = ____	5 × 9 = ____	8 × 4 = ____	4 × 9 = ____
9 × 2 = ____	4 × 6 = ____	3 × 3 = ____	6 × 5 = ____	8 × 8 = ____
7 × 6 = ____	3 × 6 = ____	6 × 4 = ____	7 × 3 = ____	8 × 9 = ____
4 × 8 = ____	7 × 9 = ____	4 × 3 = ____	3 × 7 = ____	6 × 9 = ____

D: © Joan A. Cotter 2001

Worksheet 97, The Distributive Property

Name _____

Date _____

1. Find the total area in square feet of the two rooms shown below. Solve it in two ways.

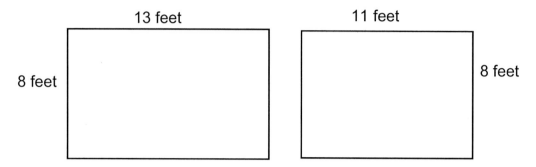

2. Alan bicycled to work 5 times last week. Each trip was 13 miles. This week he bicycled 4 times. How far did he bicycle? Solve it in two ways.

3. Angie sold 6 books in the morning and 4 books in the afternoon. Each book sold for $27. How much were her sales? Solve it in two ways.

D: © Joan A. Cotter 2001

Worksheet 98, Square Inches in a Square Foot

Name _____

Date _____

Each little square in the figure below represents one square inch. Draw a square foot, using the squares. Find the number of square inches in a square foot.

1.

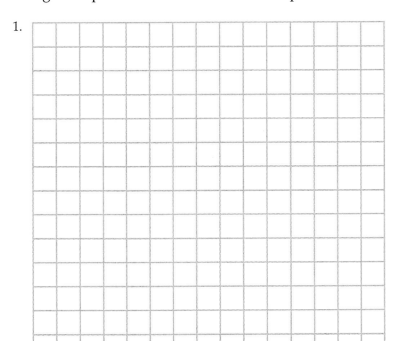

Find the number of little squares in each rectangle.

2.

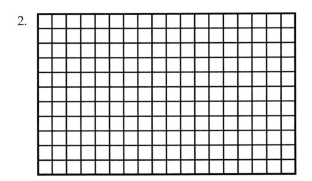

3.

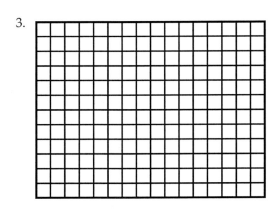

D: © Joan A. Cotter 2001

Worksheet 99, Multiplying by Two Digits

Name _____

Date _____

1. Jere bought 10 balloons at $0.75 each. What was the cost? Then Jere decided to buy 3 more balloons. What did they cost? What did the 13 balloons cost?

2. Ms. Oster is making math journals for her 27 students. Each journal has 10 sheets of white paper and 2 sheets of colored paper. How much paper does she need?

3. A person watches TV for 23 hours a week. How many hours is that in a year?

Complete the table.

Number	Number × 10	Number × 2	Number × 20	Number × 3	Number × 30
9					
11					
21					
30					
25					
100					
401					

D: © Joan A. Cotter 2001

Worksheet 100, Multiplying by Two Digits

Name _____

Date _____

Use the results of other multiplications whenever possible.

```
   49        49        49             78        78        78
 ×  4      × 50      × 54           ×  3      × 60      × 63


   61        61        61             85        85        85
 ×  2      × 80      × 82           ×  5      × 90      × 95
```

Multiply in one step.

```
   53        24        62        80        46        17
 × 32      × 14      × 26      × 96      × 43      × 35




  191       802       246       357       182       107
 × 29      × 32      × 26      × 77      × 66      × 29
```

D: © Joan A. Cotter 2001

Worksheet 101-A, Review

Name

Date _____

1. Write only the answers to the oral questions. _____ _____ _____

4. Write only the answers. $3^2 \times 4 =$ _____ $158 - 39 =$ _____ $209 + 25 =$ _____

7. Find the number of squares in the rectangle.

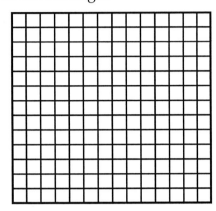

9. Ms. Garcia is buying 24 stamps, each costing 33¢. She also is buying 2 stamps for 20¢ each. What is the total cost?

11. Find the number of bars in the array.

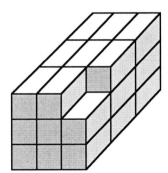

12. Write the following number: 3 million 270 thousand.

_____

13.
```
   78        78        78
  × 5       ×60       ×65
```

16.
```
  808,791        560,567
+ 352,240      −  63,945
```

D: © Joan A. Cotter 2001

Worksheet 101-B, Review

Name _____

Date _____

1. Write only the answers to the oral questions. _____ _____ _____

4. Write only the answers. $4^2 \times 2 =$ _____ $147 - 29 =$ _____ $207 + 46 =$ _____

7. Find the number of squares in the rectangle.

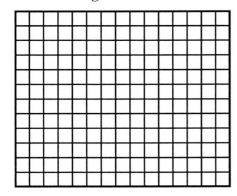

9. Mr. Johnson is buying 24 stamps each costing 34¢. He also is buying 2 stamps for 20¢ each. What is the total cost?

11. Find the number of bars in the array.

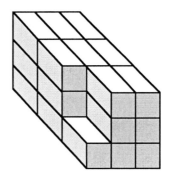

12. Write the following number: 2 million 750 thousand.

_____

13.
```
  57        57        57
 × 3      × 70      × 73
```

16.
```
  871,569          486,912
+ 352,240        −  87,374
```

D: © Joan A. Cotter 2001

Worksheet 102, Problem Solving Using a Table

Name _____

Date _____

1. Mandy wants to make equilateral triangles and squares out of toothpicks. She has 49 toothpicks and wants to make 15 figures. How many of each figure can she make?

2. Matt has eighty-two cents, all in pennies and nickels. He has two more nickels than pennies. How many pennies and nickels does he have?

3. Some children have $4.00 to buy balloons for a party. They want twice as many red balloons as blue balloons. The red balloons cost 25¢ and blue balloons cost 30¢. How many of each color can they buy?

D: © Joan A. Cotter 2001

Worksheet 103, Times Greater

Name _____

Date _____

1. Mrs. Wocky said she is 4 times older than her child, who is 8 years old. How old is Mrs. Wocky?

2. The auditorium in a school has 12 times as many seats as a classroom, which has 20 seats. How many seats are in the auditorium?

3. Many third graders can walk 3 miles in a hour. This is called walking 3 miles per hour. We write it as 3 mph. Bicyclists often travel 3 times faster than the walker. How fast is that?

4. Sometimes cars travel 8 times faster than the bicyclist. How fast is that?

5. A jet travels about 8 times faster than the car. How fast is that?

6. A racehorse can travel 15 times as fast as the child walking. How fast is that?

7. Measure the rectangle below in centimeters. What is the area?

8. Draw a rectangle 2 times longer than the rectangle at the left. What is the area? How many times greater is it?

$$\begin{array}{r}59\\\times 47\\\hline\end{array} \qquad \begin{array}{r}25\\\times 98\\\hline\end{array} \qquad \begin{array}{r}37\\\times 55\\\hline\end{array} \qquad \begin{array}{r}62\\\times 34\\\hline\end{array} \qquad \begin{array}{r}13\\\times 66\\\hline\end{array}$$

D: © Joan A. Cotter 2001

Worksheet 104, Quick Practice-Subtraction

Name _____

| Date _____ | Time _____ | Number right ____ /50 |

9 −4	16 −9	6 −4	15 −8	13 −9	5 −3	11 −6	12 −4	15 −6	13 −4
9 −6	12 −3	16 −8	8 −4	12 −6	15 −7	18 −9	6 −3	9 −5	11 −7
12 −9	14 −6	11 −8	9 −3	14 −7	15 −9	8 −3	7 −3	8 −6	11 −5
17 −8	11 −4	13 −6	11 −9	13 −7	12 −5	9 −7	13 −5	16 −7	7 −5
12 −8	17 −9	14 −8	12 −7	14 −5	11 −3	7 −4	14 −9	8 −5	13 −8

| Date _____ | Time _____ | Number right ____ /50 |

8 −6	16 −8	12 −9	9 −4	11 −6	15 −8	8 −4	11 −3	13 −4	14 −7
7 −3	17 −9	13 −5	6 −4	14 −6	13 −9	15 −6	8 −3	9 −7	14 −9
5 −3	18 −9	12 −6	12 −5	15 −7	7 −5	9 −3	11 −4	16 −9	12 −3
11 −8	13 −6	15 −9	11 −7	14 −5	9 −6	12 −8	12 −4	11 −5	13 −8
7 −4	13 −7	11 −9	17 −8	8 −5	6 −3	14 −8	9 −5	16 −7	12 −7

D: © Joan A. Cotter 2001

Worksheet 105, Combinations

Name _____

Date _____

1. Use the digits 1, 2, and 3 to write all possible 3-digit numbers using each digit once.

Which is the greatest number?   Which is the least number?

_____   _____

2. Use the digits 1, 2, 3, and 4 to write all possible 4-digit numbers using each digit once.

Which is the greatest number?   Which is the least number?

_____   _____

3. Using the 3 letters O, P, S, and T to write all possible 4-lettered words using all the letters each time. Circle the combinations that are real words.

```
   3 7        4 4        8 9        5 4        8 6
 × 5 1      × 6 6      × 6 4      × 3 6      × 6 1
```

D: © Joan A. Cotter 2001

Worksheet 106, Beginning Division

Name _____

Date _____

Add parts and numbers to the part-whole circles sets. Then write the equation.

1. Two performing partners won $18. How much did each one get?

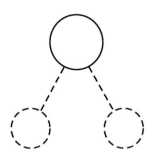

_____

2. Mrs. Czech has 2 dozen colored eggs. She is putting the same number into 4 baskets. How many will be in each basket?

_____

3. Mr. Lumba has 21 cards that he is giving out to 3 students. How many does each one get?

_____

4. A quart has 32 ounces. A quart of milk is poured into 4 glasses. How many ounces of milk are in each glass?

_____

```
   2 6        7 9        1 3        2 5        8 5
 × 1 9      × 6 1      × 6 8      × 4 2      × 7 6
```

D: © Joan A. Cotter 2001

Worksheet 107, Operations With Parts and Wholes

Name _____

Date _____

Fill in the circles and write equations. Where more than one circle is blank, make them all equal.

1.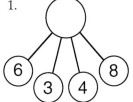
2.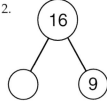
3.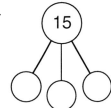
4.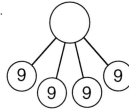

5.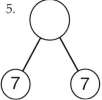
6.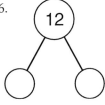
7.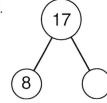
8.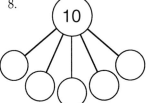

Solve these problems. Draw the part-whole circles and write the numbers and equations.

9. Quint had $5 and bought two items, costing $2.17 and $1.98. What was his change?

10. Quanda has 2 dozen decorated eggs. She is giving them to 3 friends. How many eggs does each friend receive?

```
    1 8        7 5        4 5        3 9        5 9
  × 2 8      × 5 9      × 5 2      × 2 2      × 6 5
```

D: © Joan A. Cotter 2001

Worksheet 108-A, Review

Name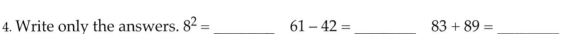

Date

1. Write only the answers to the oral questions. _____ _____ _____

4. Write only the answers. 8^2 = _____   61 – 42 = _____   83 + 89 = _____

7. A group of 3 children have 15 sheets of special paper to share. How many sheets does each one get? Complete the part-whole circle sets. Then write the equation.

9. Wen bought 2 identical parts, each costing $25.49. How much change did he get back from $60?

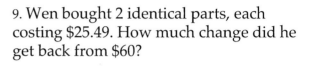

12. Draw a rectangle with the horizontal side 2 times wider than the one below. What is the area of each rectangle.

18 cm

9 cm

13. Write the largest number you can using all of these digits: 2, 7, 1, 4, 9. _____

14. Wendy is buying 17 favors. Each one cost 29¢. What is her total cost?

15. Write all the 3-digit numbers possible using 7, 8, and 9 for each number.

D: © Joan A. Cotter 2001

Worksheet 108-B, Review

Name _____

Date _____

1. Write only the answers to the oral questions. _____ _____ _____

4. Write only the answers. $6^2 =$ _____ $93 - 39 =$ _____ $76 + 89 =$ _____

7. A group of 3 children have 18 dollars to share. How much does each one get? Complete the part-whole circle sets. Then write the equation.

9. Wendi bought 2 identical gifts, costing $17.53 each. How much change did she get back from $50?

12. Draw a rectangle with the vertical side 2 times higher than the one below. What is the area of each rectangle?

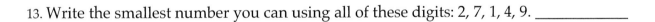

8 cm

16 cm

13. Write the smallest number you can using all of these digits: 2, 7, 1, 4, 9. _____

14. William is buying 19 favors. Each one cost 39¢. What is his total cost?

15. Write all the 3-digit numbers possible using 1, 2, and 5 for each number.

D: © Joan A. Cotter 2001

Worksheet 109, Division: Number in a Group

Name _____

Date _____

Solve these problems and explain your work. Use part-whole circles.

1. Louis is dividing 38 crayons among 5 children. How many does each one get? Are there any left over?

2. Louise did the same job for 2 days and earned $11.00. How much did Louise earn each day?

3. Four children are splitting a pizza that is cut into 6 pieces. How many pieces does each one get?

```
   7 1        9 6        3 6        5 2        9 9
 × 4 2      × 2 6      × 8 4      × 3 9      × 7 5
```

D: © Joan A. Cotter 2001

Worksheet 110, Division: Number of Groups

Name _____

Date _____

Solve these problems and explain your work.

1. Six people are needed to play on a team for a certain game. How many teams can be made with 62 people?

2. In a certain restaurant only 4 people can sit at a table. How many tables are needed for 14 people?

3. Robert needs to buy 55 candles for his grandmother's birthday cake. They are sold with ten in a package. How many packages does Lee need to buy?

4. Roberta has 33 quarters. How many dollars would she have if she exchanged the quarters for dollars?

D: © Joan A. Cotter 2001

Worksheet 111, Parts and Wholes With Number of Groups

Name _____

Date _____

Draw the parts needed for the part whole circles and write the equations.

1.
   _____

2.
   _____

3.
   _____

4.
   _____

5. 100
   25
   _____

6. 24
   8
   _____

```
  9 1 9        1 2 5        5 1 2
×   3 3      ×   1 8      ×   7 3
```

D: © Joan A. Cotter 2001

Worksheet 112, Problems Using Part-Whole

Name _____

Date _____

Complete the parts needed for the part whole circles and write the equations.

1. Barry, Carrie, and Larry each have 18 dollars. How much do they have together?

2. Barry wants to spend his $18 on books. Each book costs $6. How many books can he buy?

3. Carrie earned $24.67. How much money does she have now?

4. Carrie spent $16.32 for 4 plants. How much did each plant cost?

5. Larry spent 6 dollars and 43 cents for a gift. How much money does Larry have now?

6. Larry wants to buy 4 little gifts, which cost $2.85 each. Will he have enough money?

D: © Joan A. Cotter 2001

Worksheet 113, Dividing With Multiples-1

Name _____

Date _____

Write the multiples of 2.

_____ _____ _____ _____ _____

_____ _____ _____ _____ _____

6 ÷ 2 = ____   20 ÷ 2 = ____   2 ÷ 2 = ____   16 ÷ 2 = ____   4 ÷ 2 = ____

12 ÷ 2 = ____   14 ÷ 2 = ____   18 ÷ 2 = ____   8 ÷ 2 = ____   10 ÷ 2 = ____

Write the multiples of 4.

_____ _____ _____ _____ _____

_____ _____ _____ _____ _____

12 ÷ 4 = ____   4 ÷ 4 = ____   20 ÷ 4 = ____   28 ÷ 4 = ____   32 ÷ 4 = ____

24 ÷ 4 = ____   36 ÷ 4 = ____   16 ÷ 4 = ____   8 ÷ 4 = ____   40 ÷ 4 = ____

Write the multiples of 6.

_____ _____ _____ _____ _____

_____ _____ _____ _____ _____

12 ÷ 6 = ____   24 ÷ 6 = ____   54 ÷ 6 = ____   18 ÷ 6 = ____   42 ÷ 6 = ____

60 ÷ 6 = ____   6 ÷ 6 = ____   48 ÷ 6 = ____   36 ÷ 6 = ____   30 ÷ 6 = ____

Write the multiples of 8.

_____ _____ _____ _____ _____

_____ _____ _____ _____ _____

80 ÷ 8 = ____   8 ÷ 8 = ____   56 ÷ 8 = ____   72 ÷ 8 = ____   64 ÷ 8 = ____

48 ÷ 8 = ____   24 ÷ 8 = ____   40 ÷ 8 = ____   16 ÷ 8 = ____   32 ÷ 8 = ____

D: © Joan A. Cotter 2001

Worksheet 114-A, Review

Name _____

Date _____

1. Write only the answers to the oral questions. _____ _____ _____

4. Write only the answers. 9 squared = _____   136 – 98 = _____ $3\frac{1}{2} + 3\frac{1}{2}$ = _____

Add parts and numbers to the part-whole circles sets. Then write the equations.

7. Four sisters are sharing a dozen cookies. How many cookies does each one get?

9. Sammy pays 25¢ for a bus token. How many tokens can Sammy get for 75¢?

11. Write the multiples of 3.

_____ _____ _____

_____ _____ _____

_____ _____ _____

_____

13. Use the multiples to find the quotients.

6 ÷ 3 = _____   21 ÷ 3 = _____

18 ÷ 3 = _____   27 ÷ 3 = _____

9 ÷ 3 = _____   24 ÷ 3 = _____

3 ÷ 3 = _____   15 ÷ 3 = _____

21. 7 6 0 8
     × 7 4
     _____

22. 7 5 6 1
    + 7 6 4 9
     _____

23. 1 2 3 2
    – 1 3 5
     _____

D: © Joan A. Cotter 2001

Worksheet 114-B, Review

Name _____

Date _____

1. Write only the answers to the oral questions. _____ _____ _____

4. Write only the answers. 1 squared = _____   127 − 99 = _____ $2\frac{1}{2} + 3\frac{1}{2} =$ _____

Add parts and numbers to the part-whole circles sets. Then write the equations.

7. Three brothers are splitting a dozen cookies. How many cookies does each one get?

○

9. Silvia pays 50¢ for a bus token. How many tokens can Silvia get for $2?

○

11. Write the multiples of 4.

___ ___ ___ ___ ___

___ ___ ___ ___ ___

13. Use the multiples to find the quotients.

8 ÷ 4 = ____   20 ÷ 4 = ____

12 ÷ 4 = ____   28 ÷ 4 = ____

36 ÷ 4 = ____   24 ÷ 4 = ____

4 ÷ 4 = ____   16 ÷ 4 = ____

21.   8 4 0 9
      × 2 7
      _____

22.   8 3 4 9
    + 5 6 7 1
      _____

23.   1 4 8 3
      − 4 9 3
      _____

D: © Joan A. Cotter 2001

Worksheet 115, Two-Step Problems Using Part-Whole

Name _____

Date _____

Complete the parts needed for the part whole circles and write the equations.

1. Four people order 2 pizzas, which are cut into 8 pieces. How many pieces does each person get?

   ◯   ◯

2. Lynn practices the violin for one-half hour each day. Lynn also plays during the lesson for 60 minutes. How many hours does Lynn play the violin in a week?

   ◯   ◯

3. Jo wants to read 100 pages. Jo read 22 pages on Monday, 29 pages on Tuesday, and only 17 pages on Wednesday. How many pages does Jo still need to read?

   ◯   ◯

D: © Joan A. Cotter 2001

Worksheet 116, Dividing With Multiples

Name _____

Date _____

Write the multiples of 9.

___ ___ ___ ___ ___ ___

___ ___ ___ ___ ___ ___

What pattern do you see with the quotients in the boxes?

| 36 ÷ 9 = ___ | 54 ÷ 9 = ___ | 81 ÷ 9 = ___ | 27 ÷ 9 = ___ | 90 ÷ 9 = ___ |
| 63 ÷ 9 = ___ | 45 ÷ 9 = ___ | 18 ÷ 9 = ___ | 72 ÷ 9 = ___ | 9 ÷ 9 = ___ |

Write the multiples of 5.

___ ___

___ ___

___ ___

___ ___

___ ___

25 ÷ 5 = ___   30 ÷ 5 = ___

5 ÷ 5 = ___   45 ÷ 5 = ___

20 ÷ 5 = ___   35 ÷ 5 = ___

50 ÷ 5 = ___   10 ÷ 5 = ___

40 ÷ 5 = ___   15 ÷ 5 = ___

What pattern do you see when you divide a multiple of 10 by 5?

Write the multiples of 3.

___ ___ ___

___ ___ ___

___ ___ ___

___

21 ÷ 3 = ___   15 ÷ 3 = ___   24 ÷ 3 = ___

30 ÷ 3 = ___   3 ÷ 3 = ___   6 ÷ 3 = ___

27 ÷ 3 = ___   12 ÷ 3 = ___   18 ÷ 3 = ___

9 ÷ 3 = ___

Write the multiples of 7.

___ ___ ___

___ ___ ___

___ ___ ___

___ ___

14 ÷ 7 = ___   56 ÷ 7 = ___   42 ÷ 7 = ___

21 ÷ 7 = ___   70 ÷ 7 = ___   35 ÷ 7 = ___

49 ÷ 7 = ___   7 ÷ 7 = ___   28 ÷ 7 = ___

63 ÷ 7 = ___

D: © Joan A. Cotter 2001

Worksheet 117, Division Problems With Money

Name _____

Date _____

1. Abby, Brianna, and Carla bought a pizza for $4.68. How much money does each one need to pay? Explain your work with words and pictures.

2. Andy, Byron, Carlos, and Damian bought a pizza for $10.72? How much does each one owe? Explain your work with words and pictures.

D: © Joan A. Cotter 2001

Worksheet 118, Quick Practice-16

Name _____

| 5 10 |
| 15 20 |
| 25 30 |
| 35 40 |
| 45 50 |

| 2 4 6 8 10 |
| 12 14 16 18 20 |

| 10 20 30 40 50 |
| 60 70 80 90 100 |

Date _____

12 ÷ 2 = ____   4 ÷ 2 = ____   18 ÷ 2 = ____   8 ÷ 2 = ____   6 ÷ 2 = ____

14 ÷ 2 = ____   16 ÷ 2 = ____   2 ÷ 2 = ____   20 ÷ 2 = ____   10 ÷ 2 = ____

2 × ____ = 12   2 × ____ = 16   2 × ____ = 10   2 × ____ = 2   2 × ____ = 6

2 × ____ = 4   2 × ____ = 14   2 × ____ = 8   2 × ____ = 18   2 × ____ = 20

70 ÷ 10 = ____   30 ÷ 10 = ____   20 ÷ 10 = ____   40 ÷ 10 = ____   80 ÷ 10 = ____

Date _____

8 ÷ 2 = ____   10 ÷ 2 = ____   20 ÷ 2 = ____   12 ÷ 2 = ____   6 ÷ 2 = ____

14 ÷ 2 = ____   18 ÷ 2 = ____   16 ÷ 2 = ____   2 ÷ 2 = ____   4 ÷ 2 = ____

20 ÷ 5 = ____   50 ÷ 5 = ____   45 ÷ 5 = ____   35 ÷ 5 = ____   5 ÷ 5 = ____

30 ÷ 5 = ____   10 ÷ 5 = ____   40 ÷ 5 = ____   25 ÷ 5 = ____   15 ÷ 5 = ____

40 ÷ 10 = ____   30 ÷ 10 = ____   60 ÷ 10 = ____   70 ÷ 10 = ____   90 ÷ 10 = ____

Date _____

60 ÷ 10 = ____   6 ÷ 2 = ____   5 ÷ 5 = ____   10 ÷ 5 = ____   16 ÷ 2 = ____

10 ÷ 2 = ____   15 ÷ 5 = ____   40 ÷ 10 = ____   20 ÷ 5 = ____   25 ÷ 5 = ____

30 ÷ 10 = ____   14 ÷ 2 = ____   30 ÷ 5 = ____   90 ÷ 10 = ____   70 ÷ 10 = ____

2 ÷ 2 = ____   4 ÷ 2 = ____   35 ÷ 5 = ____   18 ÷ 2 = ____   12 ÷ 2 = ____

40 ÷ 5 = ____   45 ÷ 5 = ____   20 ÷ 2 = ____   8 ÷ 2 = ____   50 ÷ 5 = ____

D: © Joan A. Cotter 2001

Worksheet 119, The Dividing Line

Name _____

Date _____

21 ÷ 3 = ____   15 ÷ 3 = ____   12 ÷ 3 = ____   6 ÷ 3 = ____   27 ÷ 3 = ____

9 ÷ 3 = ____   3 ÷ 3 = ____   24 ÷ 3 = ____   30 ÷ 3 = ____   18 ÷ 3 = ____

$\frac{18}{3}$ = ____ $\frac{21}{3}$ = ____ $\frac{9}{3}$ = ____ $\frac{6}{3}$ = ____ $\frac{30}{3}$ = ____

$\frac{24}{3}$ = ____ $\frac{27}{3}$ = ____ $\frac{3}{3}$ = ____ $\frac{12}{3}$ = ____ $\frac{15}{3}$ = ____

$\frac{10}{2}$ = ____ $\frac{9}{2}$ = ____ $\frac{8}{2}$ = ____ $\frac{7}{2}$ = ____ $\frac{6}{2}$ = ____

$\frac{5}{2}$ = ____ $\frac{4}{2}$ = ____ $\frac{3}{2}$ = ____ $\frac{2}{2}$ = ____ $\frac{1}{2}$ = ____

What pattern do you see?

Write these two ways: with a division sign and with a dividing line. Then find the quotients.

Eighty divided by ten   Thirty divided by ten   Twenty divided by two

_____   _____   _____

_____   _____   _____

Eighteen divided by three   Twenty-one divided by three   Fourteen divided by two

_____   _____   _____

_____   _____   _____

D: © Joan A. Cotter 2001

Worksheet 120, Non-Unit Fractions

Name _____

Date _____

1. Three children are dividing two candy bars, so each person gets the same amount. How much does each one get? Explain your work with words and pictures.

2. Four children have three large cookies. How can they divide them so each person gets the same amount? Explain your work with words and pictures.

Use the fraction pieces to find the following answers.

3. How many $\frac{1}{4}$s are needed to equal 1? _____

4. How many $\frac{1}{6}$s are needed to equal 1? _____

5. How many $\frac{1}{6}$s are needed to equal $\frac{1}{2}$? _____

6. How many $\frac{1}{8}$s are needed to equal 1? _____

3. How many $\frac{1}{8}$s are needed to equal $\frac{1}{2}$? _____

Worksheet 121-A, Review

Name _____

Date _____

1. Write only the answers to the oral questions. _____ _____ _____

4. Write only the answers. $3\frac{1}{2} + 1\frac{1}{2} =$ _____ $141 - 13 =$ _____ $39 + 58 =$ _____

7. Write the fractions in the rectangles.

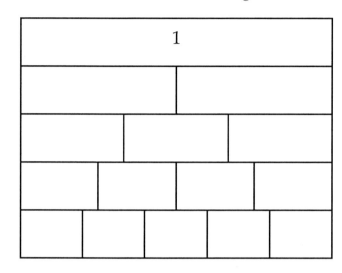

22. From these fractions, write the pairs that equal 1.

$\frac{1}{2}$ $\frac{7}{8}$ $\frac{2}{3}$ $\frac{1}{3}$ $\frac{1}{2}$ $\frac{3}{8}$ $\frac{5}{8}$ $\frac{1}{8}$

_____

_____

_____

_____

23. Write the multiples of 3.

___ ___ ___

___ ___ ___

___ ___ ___

___

33. Use the multiples to find the quotients.

$24 \div 3 =$ ___ $27 \div 3 =$ ___

$30 \div 3 =$ ___ $9 \div 3 =$ ___

$6 \div 3 =$ ___ $18 \div 3 =$ ___

$15 \div 3 =$ ___ $21 \div 3 =$ ___

34.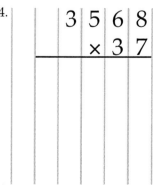
```
  3 5 6 8
×     3 7
```

35.
```
  2 8 5 6
+   8 9 4
```

36.
```
  2 8 0 2
−   4 0 4
```

D: © Joan A. Cotter 2001

Worksheet 121-B, Review

Name _____

Date _____

1. Write only the answers to the oral questions. _____ _____ _____

4. Write only the answers. $3\frac{1}{2} + 2\frac{1}{2}$ = _____   180 − 34 = _____   86 + 33 = _____

7. Write the fractions in the rectangles.

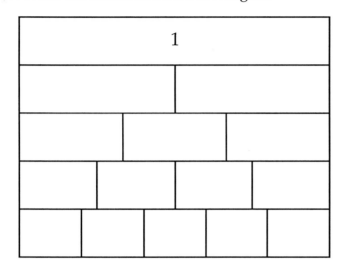

22. From these fractions, write the pairs that equal 1.

$\frac{1}{2}$ $\frac{5}{6}$ $\frac{2}{5}$ $\frac{1}{2}$ $\frac{2}{4}$ $\frac{3}{5}$ $\frac{2}{4}$ $\frac{1}{6}$

_____

_____

_____

_____

23. Write the multiples of 3.

____ ____ ____

____ ____ ____

____ ____ ____

____

33. Use the multiples to find the quotients.

9 ÷ 3 = ____   18 ÷ 3 = ____

27 ÷ 3 = ____   21 ÷ 3 = ____

15 ÷ 3 = ____   12 ÷ 3 = ____

30 ÷ 3 = ____   6 ÷ 3 = ____

34. 7 2 4 6
     × 9 2

35. 6 9 4 2
     + 7 8 9

36. 3 5 6 1
     − 8 6 4

D: © Joan A. Cotter 2001

Worksheet 122, Quick Practice-17

Name _____

5	10
15	20
25	30
35	40
45	50

| 2 | 4 | 6 | 8 | 10 |
| 12 | 14 | 16 | 18 | 20 |

| 10 | 20 | 30 | 40 | 50 |
| 60 | 70 | 80 | 90 | 100 |

Date _____

10 ÷ 2 = ____   45 ÷ 5 = ____   20 ÷ 2 = ____   40 ÷ 5 = ____   6 ÷ 2 = ____

50 ÷ 10 = ____   10 ÷ 5 = ____   8 ÷ 2 = ____   70 ÷ 10 = ____   60 ÷ 10 = ____

4 ÷ 2 = ____   40 ÷ 10 = ____   5 ÷ 5 = ____   16 ÷ 2 = ____   30 ÷ 5 = ____

25 ÷ 5 = ____   14 ÷ 2 = ____   50 ÷ 5 = ____   35 ÷ 5 = ____   90 ÷ 10 = ____

12 ÷ 2 = ____   20 ÷ 5 = ____   2 ÷ 2 = ____   18 ÷ 2 = ____   15 ÷ 5 = ____

Date _____

4 ÷ 2 = ____   50 ÷ 10 = ____   20 ÷ 5 = ____   10 ÷ 5 = ____   6 ÷ 2 = ____

5 ÷ 5 = ____   20 ÷ 2 = ____   35 ÷ 5 = ____   12 ÷ 2 = ____   8 ÷ 2 = ____

45 ÷ 5 = ____   50 ÷ 5 = ____   18 ÷ 2 = ____   25 ÷ 5 = ____   30 ÷ 5 = ____

14 ÷ 2 = ____   16 ÷ 2 = ____   40 ÷ 10 = ____   90 ÷ 10 = ____   15 ÷ 5 = ____

2 ÷ 2 = ____   60 ÷ 10 = ____   70 ÷ 10 = ____   40 ÷ 5 = ____   10 ÷ 2 = ____

Date _____

$\frac{4}{2}$ = ____ $\frac{18}{2}$ = ____ $\frac{5}{5}$ = ____ $\frac{90}{10}$ = ____ $\frac{12}{2}$ = ____

$\frac{25}{5}$ = ____ $\frac{30}{5}$ = ____ $\frac{10}{2}$ = ____ $\frac{50}{10}$ = ____ $\frac{16}{2}$ = ____

$\frac{20}{5}$ = ____ $\frac{20}{2}$ = ____ $\frac{35}{5}$ = ____ $\frac{60}{10}$ = ____ $\frac{50}{5}$ = ____

$\frac{10}{5}$ = ____ $\frac{2}{2}$ = ____ $\frac{14}{2}$ = ____ $\frac{45}{5}$ = ____ $\frac{15}{5}$ = ____

$\frac{70}{10}$ = ____ $\frac{6}{2}$ = ____ $\frac{40}{10}$ = ____ $\frac{40}{5}$ = ____ $\frac{8}{2}$ = ____

D: © Joan A. Cotter 2001

Worksheet 123, Comparing Fractions

Name _____

Date _____

Write <, >, or = in the circles.

5 ◯ 7   3 ◯ 2   4 ◯ 8

$\frac{1}{5}$ ◯ $\frac{1}{7}$ $\frac{1}{3}$ ◯ $\frac{1}{2}$ $\frac{1}{4}$ ◯ $\frac{1}{8}$

$\frac{2}{5}$ ◯ $\frac{2}{7}$ $\frac{2}{3}$ ◯ $\frac{2}{2}$ $\frac{2}{4}$ ◯ $\frac{2}{8}$

10. Color $\frac{2}{6}$ and $\frac{2}{7}$ green. Which is more? _____

11. Color $\frac{2}{4}$ and $\frac{1}{2}$ blue. Which is more? _____

12. Color $\frac{3}{3}$ and 1 red. Which is more? _____

13. Color $\frac{8}{9}$ and $\frac{9}{10}$ yellow. Which is more? _____

Circle which is more?

14. $\frac{1}{6}$ $\frac{1}{7}$ $\frac{1}{8}$

15. $\frac{2}{3}$ $\frac{2}{4}$ $\frac{2}{5}$

Circle which is less?

16. $\frac{1}{6}$ $\frac{2}{6}$ $\frac{3}{6}$

17. $\frac{7}{8}$ $\frac{8}{8}$ $\frac{9}{8}$

18. There are 3 glasses of chocolate milk to be divided among 6 children. Ben says each child will get $\frac{3}{6}$ of a glass each. Beth says each one will get $\frac{1}{2}$. Who is right? Explain your answer.

D: © Joan A. Cotter 2001

Worksheet 124, The Ruler Chart

Name _____

Date _____

Write the fraction value at the top of each line. Use the Ruler Chart for playing the Ruler Game and for completing the answers below.

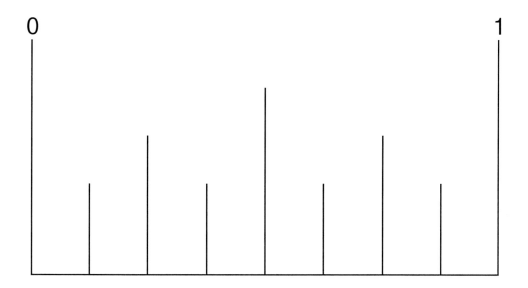

Write <, >, or = in the circles.

$\frac{5}{8}$ ◯ $\frac{7}{8}$ $\frac{1}{4}$ ◯ $\frac{1}{8}$ $\frac{2}{4}$ ◯ $\frac{1}{2}$

$\frac{4}{4}$ ◯ 1 $\frac{3}{8}$ ◯ $\frac{1}{4}$ $\frac{3}{4}$ ◯ $\frac{5}{8}$

1 ◯ $\frac{2}{2}$ $\frac{3}{8}$ ◯ $\frac{3}{4}$ $\frac{4}{8}$ ◯ $\frac{2}{4}$

Circle the greatest fraction in each row.

14.	$\frac{3}{4}$	$\frac{5}{8}$	$\frac{1}{2}$
15.	$\frac{2}{8}$	$\frac{2}{4}$	$\frac{2}{2}$

Use the fractions from the Ruler Chart to answer these questions. Some have more than one answer.

Name a fraction less than $\frac{1}{4}$. _____

Name a fraction greater than $\frac{5}{8}$. _____

Name a fraction equal to $\frac{6}{8}$. _____

Name a fraction more than $\frac{1}{4}$ but less than $\frac{1}{2}$. _____

Name a fraction more than $\frac{1}{2}$ but less than $\frac{7}{8}$. _____

D: © Joan A. Cotter 2001

Worksheet 125, Fraction Problems

Name _____

Date _____

1. Kelsey spent $\frac{3}{4}$ of her allowance. What fraction did she have left? Her allowance is $4. How much did she have left? How much did she spend?

2. Kyle had $\frac{7}{8}$ of his math problems correct. What fraction did he have wrong? There are 24 problems. How many did he have right? How many did he have wrong?

3. Keith wants to know his pulse–how many times his heart beats in a minute. He counted 20 beats in a fourth of a minute. How many beats is that per minute?

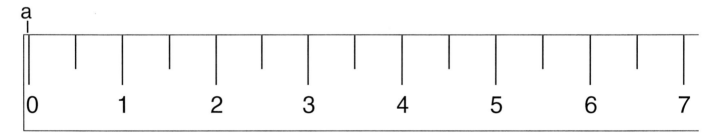

An ant is walking back and forth on the ruler above.

The ant starts at 0. Write an *a* there.

The ant moves $1\frac{1}{2}$ inches to the right. Write a *t* at this point.

Next the ant moves to the left 1 inch. Write an *n*.

This time the ant goes for a longer walk of $5\frac{1}{2}$ inches to the right. Write an *e*.

Now the ant turns around and walks left $\frac{4}{2}$ inches. Write an *a*.

The ant continues left $\frac{3}{2}$ inches. Write an *e*.

Once more the ant changes directions. This time the ant walks half of 5 inches. Write a *t*.

For the last time the ant runs to the right three times, each time $\frac{1}{2}$ inch. Write *r*.

What animal spies the ant? _____

D: © Joan A. Cotter 2001

Worksheet 126, Quick Practice-18

Name _____

Date _____

30 ÷ 5 = ___	8 ÷ 2 = ___	16 ÷ 2 = ___	20 ÷ 5 = ___	35 ÷ 5 = ___
10 ÷ 2 = ___	25 ÷ 5 = ___	45 ÷ 5 = ___	4 ÷ 2 = ___	2 ÷ 2 = ___
50 ÷ 5 = ___	6 ÷ 2 = ___	10 ÷ 5 = ___	20 ÷ 2 = ___	15 ÷ 5 = ___
40 ÷ 5 = ___	12 ÷ 2 = ___	18 ÷ 2 = ___	5 ÷ 5 = ___	14 ÷ 2 = ___

Date _____

3)3̄	2)4̄	3)2̄4̄	3)6̄	2)1̄0̄
3)1̄5̄	3)1̄8̄	2)2̄0̄	2)2̄	3)2̄1̄
3)3̄0̄	2)1̄6̄	2)1̄4̄	3)9̄	2)6̄
2)1̄2̄	3)2̄7̄	3)1̄2̄	2)8̄	2)1̄8̄

Date _____

3)2̄1̄	2)2̄0̄	3)2̄4̄	3)3̄0̄	2)6̄
2)1̄4̄	3)1̄2̄	2)1̄2̄	2)8̄	3)2̄7̄
2)1̄6̄	3)3̄	3)1̄5̄	2)2̄	3)9̄
3)6̄	2)4̄	2)1̄0̄	3)1̄8̄	2)1̄8̄

D: © Joan A. Cotter 2001

Worksheet 127, The Division "House"

Name _____

Date _____

Write the multiples of 3.

____ ____ ____   3)6̄   3)1̄2̄   3)2̄7̄   3)3̄0̄

____ ____ ____   3)2̄1̄   3)1̄8̄   3)1̄5̄   3)9̄

____ ____ ____   3)2̄4̄   3)3̄   3)2̄1̄   3)1̄8̄

____

Write each division problem and answer three ways.

40 ÷ 5 = ____	$\frac{40}{5}$	5)4̄0̄
18 ÷ 2 = ____		
	$\frac{21}{3}$	
		3)1̄8̄
18 ÷ 2 = ____		
	$\frac{14}{2}$	
		5)2̄5̄
12 ÷ 2 = ____		
	$\frac{12}{3}$	
		3)2̄4̄

D: © Joan A. Cotter 2001

Worksheet 128, Division Remainders in Context

Name _____

Date _____

1. Thirteen people are going to a concert. Four will fit in a car. How many cars will be needed?

2. Patsy is planting petunias in rows, with only 4 in a row. She has 13 plants. How many rows can she plant?

3. Four girls earn $13. They divide it evenly. How much does each one get?

4. Four boys are splitting 13 miniature candy bars. They divide them evenly. How much does each one get?

5. Jack is packing cookies 4 to a bag. He has 13 cookies to pack. He gets to eat any leftover cookies. How many cookies does he eat?

6. What is the same about these five problems? What is different about them?

D: © Joan A. Cotter 2001

Worksheet 129-A, Review

Name _____

Date _____

1. Write only the answers to the oral questions. _____ _____ _____

4. Write only the answers. $\frac{1}{2}$ of 3 = _____   142 – 71 = _____   89 + 91 = _____

7. Fourteen children are eating at a banquet. Four will fit at a table. How many tables will be needed?

9. Paul is building stools, with three legs each. He has 19 legs. How many stools can he build?

11. Paula wants to know her pulse–how many times her heart beats in a minute–after running. She counted 30 beats in a fourth of a minute. How many beats is that per minute?

13. Write the missing fractions.

21. Write <, >, or = in the circles.

$\frac{1}{2}\bigcirc\frac{3}{8}$ $\frac{3}{8}\bigcirc\frac{3}{4}$

$\frac{1}{4}\bigcirc\frac{3}{4}$ $\frac{1}{2}\bigcirc\frac{2}{4}$

25. Write each division problem and answer three ways.

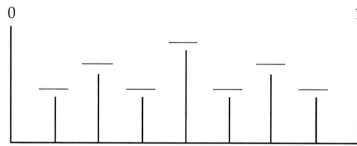

D: © Joan A. Cotter 2001

Worksheet 129-B, Review

Name _____

Date _____

1. Write only the answers to the oral questions. _____ _____ _____

4. Write only the answers. $\frac{1}{2}$ of 5 = _____   185 − 34 = _____   78 + 82 = _____

7. Seventeen children are riding on a chairlift. Three will fit on a chair. How many chairs will they need?

9. Roberta is building tables, with four legs each. She has 21 legs. How many tables can she build?

11. Roberto wants to know his pulse–how many times his heart beats in a minute–after running. He counted 41 beats in a third of a minute. How many beats is that per minute?

13. Write the missing fractions.

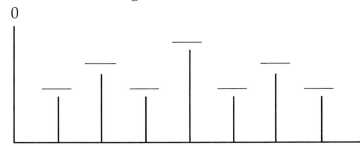

21. Write <, >, or = in the circles.

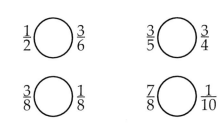

25. Write each division problem and answer three ways.

15 ÷ 3 = _____
$\frac{18}{2}$
5)$\overline{25}$

D: © Joan A. Cotter 2001

Worksheet 130, Quick Practice-19

Name _____

Date _____ Time _____ Number right _____

$\frac{6}{3}$ = ____ $\frac{10}{2}$ = ____ $\frac{30}{5}$ = ____ $\frac{12}{3}$ = ____ $\frac{50}{5}$ = ____ $\frac{9}{3}$ = ____

$\frac{45}{5}$ = ____ $\frac{18}{2}$ = ____ $\frac{4}{2}$ = ____ $\frac{20}{5}$ = ____ $\frac{18}{3}$ = ____ $\frac{20}{2}$ = ____

$\frac{25}{5}$ = ____ $\frac{5}{5}$ = ____ $\frac{27}{3}$ = ____ $\frac{12}{2}$ = ____ $\frac{40}{5}$ = ____ $\frac{15}{5}$ = ____

$\frac{8}{2}$ = ____ $\frac{16}{2}$ = ____ $\frac{24}{3}$ = ____ $\frac{2}{2}$ = ____ $\frac{30}{3}$ = ____ $\frac{10}{5}$ = ____

$\frac{21}{3}$ = ____ $\frac{6}{2}$ = ____ $\frac{3}{3}$ = ____ $\frac{15}{3}$ = ____ $\frac{14}{2}$ = ____ $\frac{35}{5}$ = ____

Date _____ Time _____ Number right _____

$\frac{12}{2}$ = ____ $\frac{5}{5}$ = ____ $\frac{6}{2}$ = ____ $\frac{6}{3}$ = ____ $\frac{40}{5}$ = ____ $\frac{35}{5}$ = ____

$\frac{20}{5}$ = ____ $\frac{27}{3}$ = ____ $\frac{45}{5}$ = ____ $\frac{3}{3}$ = ____ $\frac{15}{3}$ = ____ $\frac{10}{5}$ = ____

$\frac{30}{3}$ = ____ $\frac{18}{2}$ = ____ $\frac{50}{5}$ = ____ $\frac{15}{5}$ = ____ $\frac{21}{3}$ = ____ $\frac{12}{3}$ = ____

$\frac{18}{3}$ = ____ $\frac{2}{2}$ = ____ $\frac{30}{5}$ = ____ $\frac{14}{2}$ = ____ $\frac{9}{3}$ = ____ $\frac{16}{2}$ = ____

$\frac{4}{2}$ = ____ $\frac{24}{3}$ = ____ $\frac{25}{5}$ = ____ $\frac{10}{2}$ = ____ $\frac{20}{2}$ = ____ $\frac{8}{2}$ = ____

Date _____ Time _____ Number right _____

$\frac{30}{3}$ = ____ $\frac{27}{3}$ = ____ $\frac{10}{2}$ = ____ $\frac{12}{3}$ = ____ $\frac{12}{2}$ = ____ $\frac{10}{5}$ = ____

$\frac{6}{2}$ = ____ $\frac{9}{3}$ = ____ $\frac{50}{5}$ = ____ $\frac{15}{5}$ = ____ $\frac{2}{2}$ = ____ $\frac{8}{2}$ = ____

$\frac{25}{5}$ = ____ $\frac{6}{3}$ = ____ $\frac{14}{2}$ = ____ $\frac{24}{3}$ = ____ $\frac{20}{2}$ = ____ $\frac{15}{3}$ = ____

$\frac{35}{5}$ = ____ $\frac{3}{3}$ = ____ $\frac{16}{2}$ = ____ $\frac{4}{2}$ = ____ $\frac{45}{5}$ = ____ $\frac{20}{5}$ = ____

$\frac{18}{2}$ = ____ $\frac{18}{3}$ = ____ $\frac{5}{5}$ = ____ $\frac{40}{5}$ = ____ $\frac{21}{3}$ = ____ $\frac{30}{5}$ = ____

D: © Joan A. Cotter 2001

Worksheet 131, Graphing Growth

Name _____

Date _____

Aster and Pansy are pets, which grow every day. Aster is $\frac{1}{4}$ inch long and Pansy is 2 inches long on Day 1. Aster doubles its length every day. Pansy grows $\frac{1}{2}$ inch day.

Fill in the table to show how the pets grow. Then graph the first 6 days.

	Day 1	Day 2	Day 3	Day 4	Day 5	Day 6	Day 7	Day 8
Aster								
Pansy								

Which day are the pets the same length? _____

Which pet will be longer on Day 10? _____

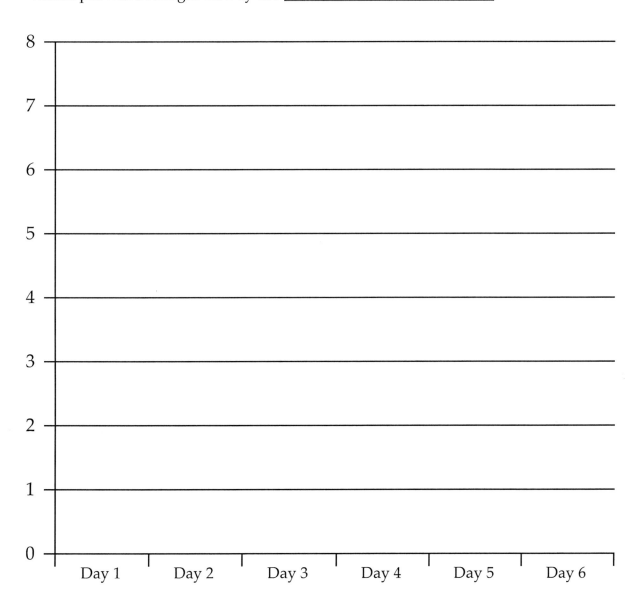

D: © Joan A. Cotter 2001

Worksheet 132, Reading a Graph on Population

Name _____

Date _____

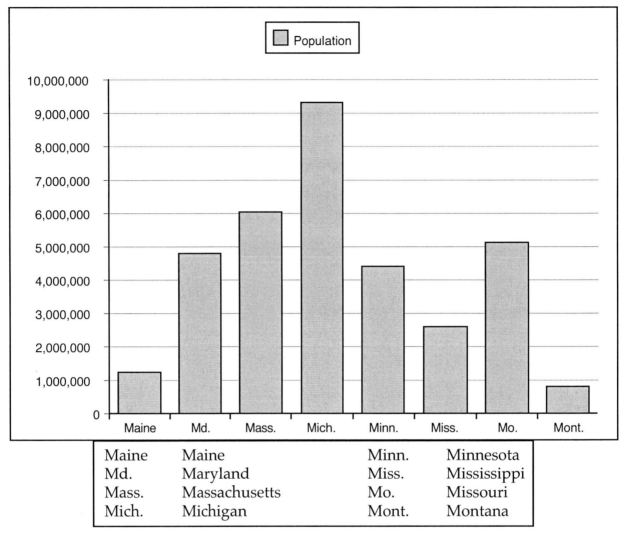

Maine	Maine	Minn.	Minnesota
Md.	Maryland	Miss.	Mississippi
Mass.	Massachusetts	Mo.	Missouri
Mich.	Michigan	Mont.	Montana

1. Which state has a population of 1,200,000?

2. Which state has a population of 4,300,000?

3. Which state has a population less than 1 million and what is the population?

4. What is the population of the state with the greatest population?

5. What is the population of Mississippi?

6. What state has twice the population of Mississippi and what is the population?

7. Which state has a population closest to Missouri and what is the population?

8. What is the difference in population between Massachusetts and Michigan?

D: © Joan A. Cotter 2001

Worksheet 133, Reading a Graph on Area

Name _____

Date _____

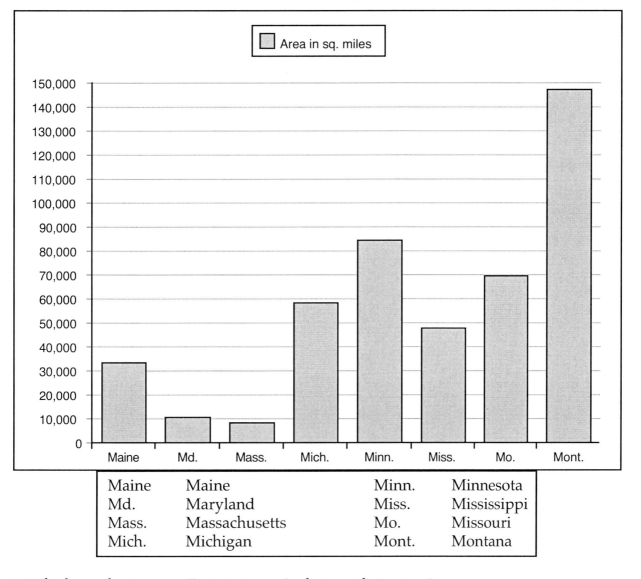

1. Which are the two smallest states and what are their sizes?

2. Which state is closest to having 50,000 square miles and what is its size?

3. What is the second largest state and what is its size?

4. Would Missouri and Michigan fit in Montana at the same time? Explain.

5. What state is nearest in size to Maine and Maryland together?

D: © Joan A. Cotter 2001

Worksheet 134, Drawing Lines and Rectangles

Name _____

Date _____

Mark the bottom line every $\frac{1}{4}$ inch; the first two are done for you. Then start at your mark and draw vertical lines between the two horizontal lines.

Mark the left line every $\frac{1}{4}$ inch; the first two are done for you. Then start at your mark and draw horizontal lines between the two vertical lines.

Draw a rectangle 4 by 2 inches on the dotted line. Draw in the square inches.

What is the area? _____

Draw the diagonals.
How long are they? _____

D: © Joan A. Cotter 2001

Worksheet 135, Drawing Diagonals

Name _____

Date _____

Draw a square on the dotted line that is 5 centimeters on a side.

What is the area in square centimeters? _____

What is the area in square inches? _____

Use your T-square and 45° triangle to draw the lines.

Draw 1 diagonal and write the fractions the square is divided into. How many right-angled triangles do you see? _____

Draw 2 diagonals and write the fractions the square is divided into. How many right-angled triangles do you see? (Hint: There are 2 different sizes.) _____

Divide the square into eighths and write the fractions. How many right-angled triangles do you see? _____

D: © Joan A. Cotter 2001

Worksheet 136-A, Review

Name _____

Date _____

1. Write only the answers to the oral questions. _____ _____ _____

4. Write only the answers. 34 × 10 = _____   152 − 26 = _____   199 + 3 = _____

3. Write the missing fractions.

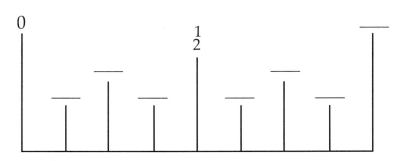

11. Write <, >, or = in the circles.

15.
$18 \div 2 =$ ____ $8 \div 2 =$ ____

$2 \div 2 =$ ____ $15 \div 3 =$ ____

$45 \div 5 =$ ____ $20 \div 5 =$ ____

$15 \div 5 =$ ____ $40 \div 5 =$ ____

23. Draw two diagonals in the rectangle.

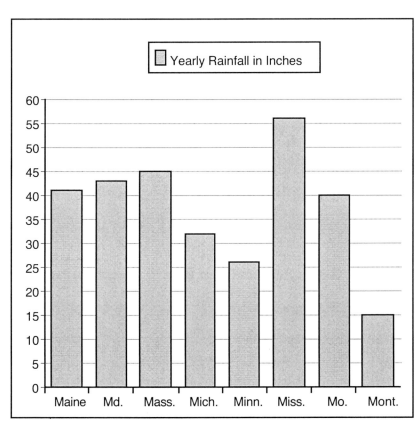

Use the chart to find the answers.

24. Which state receives 43 inches of rain? _____

25. How much rain does Minn. get? _____

26. Which state gets about twice as much rain as Mont.? _____

D: © Joan A. Cotter 2001

Worksheet 136-B, Review

Name _____

Date _____

1. Write only the answers to the oral questions. _____ _____ _____

4. Write only the answers. 65 × 10 = _____   175 − 38 = _____   198 + 4 = _____

3. Write the missing fractions.

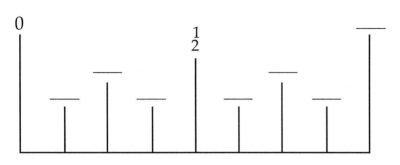

11. Write <, >, or = in the circles.

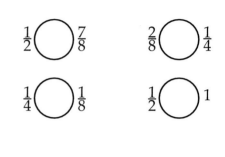

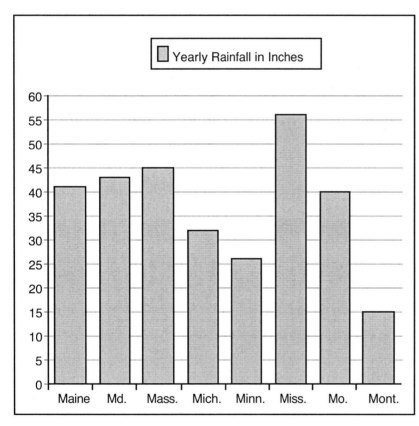

15.
18 ÷ 3 = ____   30 ÷ 5 = ____

12 ÷ 3 = ____   21 ÷ 3 = ____

45 ÷ 5 = ____   35 ÷ 5 = ____

12 ÷ 2 = ____   18 ÷ 2 = ____

23. Draw two diagonals in the quadrilateral.

Use the chart to find the answers.

24. Which state receives 41 inches of rain? _____

25. How much rain does Miss. get? _____

26. Which state gets 3 times as much rain as Mont.? _____

D: © Joan A. Cotter 2001

Worksheet 137, Drawing Octagons

Name _____

Date _____

Use your T-square and 45 triangle to construct what is shown in the little pictures.

Color $\frac{3}{8}$ of the circle red and $\frac{1}{4}$ another color. What fraction is not colored? _____

How many squares do you see? _____
Color the right-angled triangles. Color the octagon another color.

What figure did you draw? _____

Write the word to make it a traffic sign. _____

How many sets of parallel lines? _____
Color the design.

Make and color your own design.

Make and color your own design.

Make and color your own design.

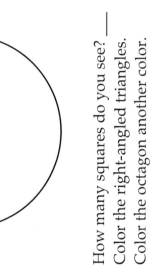
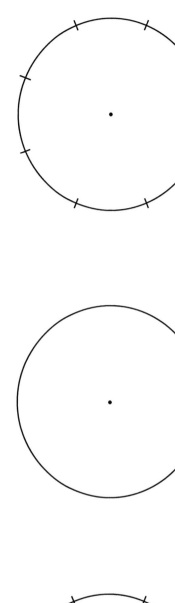

D: © Joan A. Cotter 2001

Worksheet 138, Drawing Hexagons

Name _____

Date _____

Use your T-square and 30-60 triangle to construct what is shown in the little pictures.

Color $\frac{1}{4}$ of the circle red and $\frac{1}{2}$ another color. What fraction is not colored? _____

How many small triangles? _____
How many medium triangles? _____
How many large triangles? _____

What figures did you draw? _____

Color each $\frac{1}{3}$ a different color.

How many sets of parallel lines? _____
Color the design.

How many small triangles? _____
How many large triangles? _____

Make and color your own design.

D: © Joan A. Cotter 2001

Worksheet 139, Drawing Congruent Copies

Name _____

Date _____

Use your drawing tools to make exact copies without measuring. Work carefully.

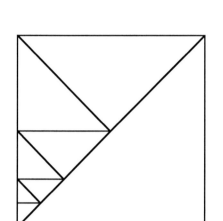

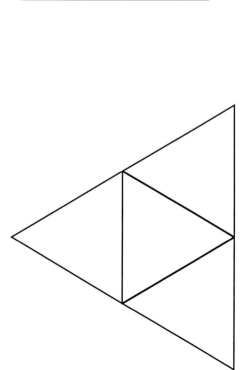

On this line construct a congruent copy of the figure on the left

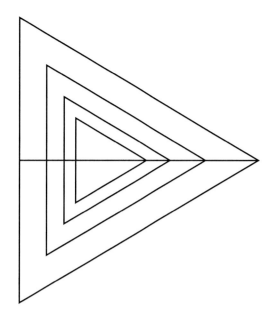

On this line construct a congruent copy of the figure on the right.

On this line construct a congruent copy of the figure above.

D: © Joan A. Cotter 2001

Worksheet 140, Drawing New Fractions

Name _____

Date _____

A fraction of a figure is shown. Use your drawing tools to make the new fraction. Explain your work. Work carefully.

$\frac{1}{2}$

Draw 1, the whole.

$\frac{2}{3}$

Draw $\frac{1}{3}$.

$\frac{2}{4}$

Draw 1, the whole.

$\frac{3}{4}$

Draw $\frac{2}{4}$.

D: © Joan A. Cotter 2001

Worksheet 141, Drawing Symmetrical Figures

Name _____

Date _____

Make the following figures symmetrical. The center lines (— — —) are the lines of symmetry. Use your drawing tools.

Make your own symmetrical designs. Use the lines of symmetry.

Use only the top edge of your T-square.

D: © Joan A. Cotter 2001

Worksheet 142-A, Review

Name _____

Date _____

1. Write only the answers to the oral questions. _____ _____ _____

4. Write only the answers. $2\frac{1}{4} + 1\frac{3}{4} =$ _____ $135 - 56 =$ _____ $23 \times 10 =$ _____

Use the letter of the figure to answer the questions below.

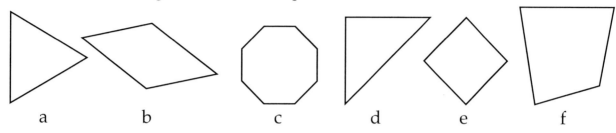

a   b   c   d   e   f

7. Which figure is an octagon? _____

8. Which figures are quadrilaterals? _____

9. Which figure are parallelograms? _____

10. Which figure is a rectangle? _____

11. Which figures have parallel lines? _____

12. $3\overline{)24}$ $2\overline{)14}$

$5\overline{)35}$ $3\overline{)18}$

$2\overline{)18}$ $5\overline{)45}$

$9\overline{)18}$ $5\overline{)30}$

20. Apples cost 89¢ a pound and grapes cost $1.67 a pound. What is the total cost of 3 pounds of apples and 4 pounds of grapes?

23. Draw freehand the figure representing 1.

24. Complete the figure freehand so it is symmetrical about the dotted line.

D: © Joan A. Cotter 2001

Worksheet 142-B, Review

Name _____

Date _____

1. Write only the answers to the oral questions. _____ _____ _____

4. Write only the answers. $2\frac{1}{3} + 2\frac{2}{3}$ = _____   141 − 85 = _____   39 × 10 = _____

Use the letter of the figure to answer the questions below.

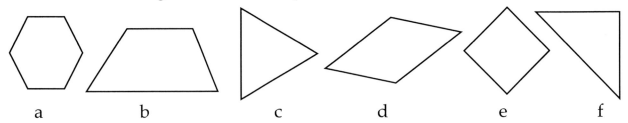

a   b   c   d   e   f

7. Which figure is an rectangle? _____

8. Which figures are quadrilaterals? _____

9. Which figure are parallelograms? _____

10. Which figure is a hexagon? _____

11. Which figures have parallel lines? _____

12. $5\overline{)25}$ $3\overline{)27}$

   $9\overline{)90}$ $2\overline{)14}$

   $4\overline{)4}$ $3\overline{)15}$

   $2\overline{)16}$ $5\overline{)40}$

20. Bananas cost 39¢ a pound and peaches cost $1.85 a pound. What is the total cost of 4 pounds of bananas and 5 pounds of peaches?

23. Draw freehand the figure representing 1.

24. Complete the figure freehand so it is symmetrical about the dotted line.

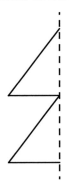

D: © Joan A. Cotter 2001

Worksheet 143, Tenths of a Centimeter

Name _____

Date _____

What are these inches divided into?   What are these inches divided into?

_____   _____

How can you tell? _____

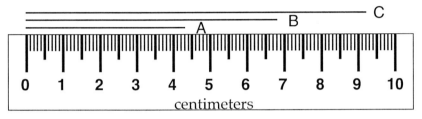

What are these centimeters divided into? _____

Line A is $4\frac{3}{10}$ cm long. How long is line B? _____   How long is line C? _____

Measure the polygons you made in the last lesson. Show your work below.

Polygon	Sketch the polygon	Length of side in cm	Number of sides	Perimeter
Equilateral triangle				
Square				
Hexagon				
Octagon				

D: © Joan A. Cotter 2001

Worksheet 144, Building a Box

Name _____

Date _____

Construct the box pattern on the line below similar to the miniature box pattern shown.

Then cut out the pattern, fold on the lines, and make the box, using tape.

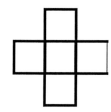

D: © Joan A. Cotter 2001

Worksheet 145, Congruent Shapes

Name _____
Date _____

Color all the congruent shapes the same color.

How many different shapes are there? _____

How many shapes of each color are there? _____

What is special about these numbers? _____

What are the areas in sq. cm of each shape? _____

What are the perimeters in cm of each shape? _____

D: © Joan A. Cotter 2001

Worksheet 146, Combining Five Squares

Name

Date

Draw freehand all 12 different shapes that can be made with 5 squares. Each square must touch another square along at least one side.

Worksheet 147, Building More Boxes

Name

Date

1. Use your drawing tools to draw one of the shapes made with five squares. Make each side of the squares 2 in. Plan ahead so it will fit on your paper.

2. Answer this question. Do you think it will make a box? _____

3. Then cut it out, fold on the lines, and see if you have a box.

D: © Joan A. Cotter 2001

Worksheet 148, Building a 4 × 3 × 1 Box

Name
Date

Make a box to fit this arrangement of cubes.

Worksheet 149, Building a 3 × 2 × 2 Box

Name
Date

Make a box to fit this arrangement of cubes.

D: © Joan A. Cotter 2001

Worksheet 150, Scaling

Name _____

Date _____

Draw the dog house to a larger scale, using the larger squares. First draw dots to show the beginning and end of each line. Then use your drawing tools to draw the lines. Draw the curve freehand.

Use a 45 triangle and a T-square upside down. Draw 3 lines parallel to the line shown. Start at the dot and make each line about an inch long.

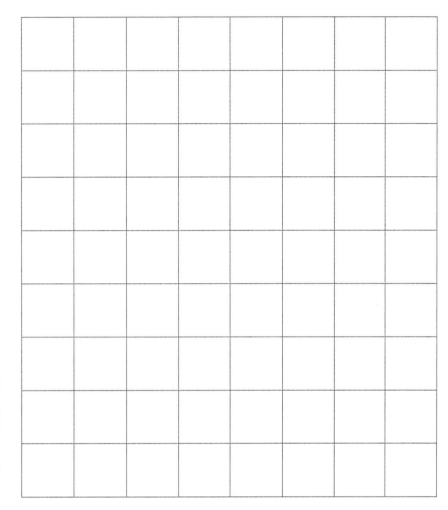

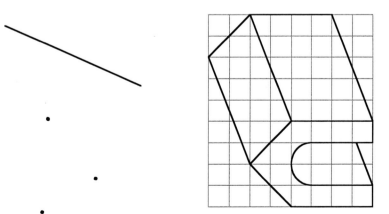

D: © Joan A. Cotter 2001

Worksheet 151-A, Review

Name _____

Date _____

1. Write only the answers to the oral questions. _____ _____ _____

4. Write only the answers. $2\frac{3}{10} + 3\frac{7}{10} =$ _____ $151 - 68 =$ _____ $92 + 98 =$ _____

7. Circle the groups of squares that are congruent with the shaded group on the left.

8. Circle the groups of squares that could make a box.

9. Draw lines to match the definitions with the words.

A triangle with 2 congruent sides.	equation
A triangle with 3 congruent sides.	equilateral triangle
A statement that two things are the same.	isosceles triangle
The answer after dividing.	quotient
A square that measures 1 inch on each side.	product
The answer after multiplying.	octagon
A polygon with 6 sides.	hexagon
A polygon with 8 sides.	square inch

18. While on a field trip, the teacher bought treats for 18 people. Each treat cost 59¢. What was the total cost? What was the change from $15? What bills and coins did the teacher receive?

D: © Joan A. Cotter 2001

Worksheet 151-B, Review

Name _____

Date _____

1. Write only the answers to the oral questions. _____ _____ _____

4. Write only the answers. $4\frac{6}{10} + 3\frac{4}{10}$ = _____   175 − 38 = _____   83 + 87 = _____

7. Circle the groups of squares that are congruent with the shaded group on the left.

8. Circle the groups of squares that could make a box.

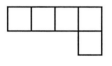 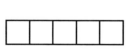 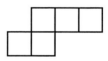

9. Draw lines to match the definitions with the words.

A polygon with 3 sides.	equation
A polygon with 4 sides.	triangle
A polygon with 6 sides.	quadrilateral
A polygon with 8 sides.	quotient
A statement that two things are the same.	product
The answer after dividing.	hexagon
The answer after multiplying.	octagon
A cube that measures 1 inch on all sides.	cubic inch

18. For a family party, Chris bought treats for 16 people. Each treat cost 79¢. What was the total cost? What was the change from $15? What bills and coins did Chris receive?

D: © Joan A. Cotter 2001

Worksheet Math Puzzles-1

Name _____

Math Puzzles-1

Fill in the missing blanks. The sum of the first three numbers in a row equals the last number in that row. The sum of the first three numbers in a column equals the last number in that column. Check your puzzle when you are done by adding all the rows and columns.

1.

3	5		9
	2	4	12
3	8	5	
12		10	37

2.

	5	1	12
7			17
6		3	
19	14	9	42

3.

3		9	16
9	7	11	
13	8		33
	19		76

4.

11		8	
	7	9	30
9		7	28
34	25		83

5.

7	6		
10		12	31
	8	9	23
	23		71

6.

8		8	22
		12	30
6			16
	22	22	68

D: © Joan A. Cotter 2001

Worksheet Math Puzzles-2

Name _____

Math Puzzles-2

Fill in the missing blanks. The sum of the first three numbers in a row equals the last number in that row. The sum of the first three numbers in a column equals the last number in that column. Check your puzzle when you are done by adding all the rows and columns.

1.

	9	1	
4	7	3	14
5		6	15
	20		44

2.

4	4		9
10	6		17
	4	12	19
	14	14	

3.

	4	12	22
7			18
4		5	10
	12	21	

4.

	10	1	
12	3		24
3			12
	15	17	53

5.

5		3	15
	3		8
6	11	6	
15			46

6.

	12	12	30
		6	25
	10		16
	33	20	71

D: © Joan A. Cotter 2001

Review First Quarter, page 1

Name _____

Date _____

Draw the hands.   Write the time two ways.

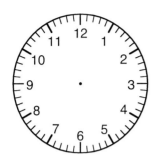   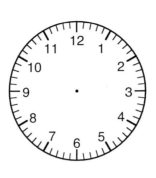   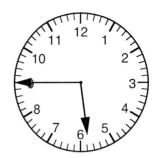

five before 3   11:05

_____

_____

Show $4\frac{1}{2}$ inches on the ruler. Circle or shade it.

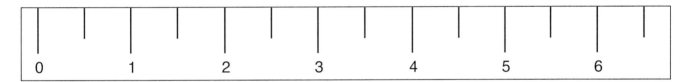

How long is this line in inches? $3\frac{1}{2}$ 2   4 $5\frac{1}{2}$
Circle your answer.

Add these. Write only the answers.   Subtract these. Write only the answers.

45 + 25 = _____   37 − 33 = _____

47 + 19 = _____   60 − 49 = _____

105 + 15 = _____   101 − 2 = _____

Write the multiples of 6.   Use the 6 table to find the answers.

___ ___ ___ ___ ___   6 × 4 = _____

___ ___ ___ ___ ___   6 × 10 = _____

What pattern do you see with the ones?   6 × 6 = _____

D: © Joan A. Cotter 2001

Test Review First Quarter, page 2

Name _____

Alex earned $3.45 on each of five days. How much money did Alex earn?

Students measured a room that is in the shape of a rectangle. One side is 389" and the second side is 176". Draw a sketch. What is the perimeter?

Write the missing amounts and the words in the rectangles below.

100¢ dollar										
___¢ _____						___¢ _____				
___¢ _____		___¢ _____			___¢ _____			___¢ _____	
___¢	___¢	___¢	___¢	___¢	___¢	___¢	___¢	___¢	___¢	___¢

Chris had five quarters and received two dollars as a gift. How money does Chris have now?

Write the missing words and number of ounces in the rectangles below.

_____ ____ oz				
half gallon	____ oz	_____		____ oz
quart	32 oz	____ oz	____ oz	____ oz

Name _____

Date _____

Draw the hands.   Write the time two ways.

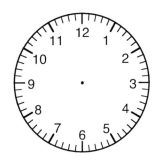   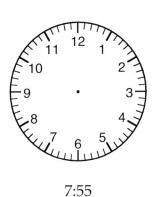   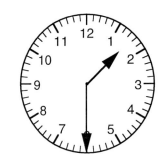

five after 8   7:55   _____

                                                  _____

Show $3\frac{1}{2}$ inches on the ruler. Circle or shade it.

How long is this line in inches? $6\frac{1}{2}$ 4   2 $2\frac{1}{2}$
Circle your answer.

Add these. Write only the answers.   Subtract these. Write only the answers.

   25 + 35 = _____   28 − 25 = _____

   47 + 28 = _____   70 − 58 = _____

   135 + 15 = _____   100 − 3 = _____

Write the multiples of 8.   Use the 8 table to find the answers.

____ ____ ____ ____ ____   8 × 3 = _____

____ ____ ____ ____ ____   8 × 9 = _____

What pattern do you see with the ones?   8 × 7 = _____

Test First Quarter, page 2

Name _____

Sammy bought four books. Each one cost $2.65. What was the total cost?

Some third graders measured a room and found all the sides measured 254 inches. What is the shape of the room? What is the perimeter?

Write the missing fractions and the amounts in the rectangles below.

___ ___¢	
___ ___¢	___ ___¢
$\frac{1}{4}$ 25¢	___ ___¢	___ ___¢	___ ___¢
$\frac{1}{10}$ 10¢	___¢	___¢	___¢	___¢	___¢	___¢	___¢	___¢	___¢

Jamie had 11 dimes and received three dollars as a gift. How much money does Jamie have now?

Write the missing fractions and the number of minutes in the rectangles below.

__ hr _____ min	
$\frac{1}{2}$ hr _____ min	__ hr _____ min
__ hr ___ min	__ hr ___ min	__ hr ___ min	__ hr ___ min

D: © Joan A. Cotter 2001

Name _____

Date _____

1. Write only the answers to the oral questions. _____ _____ _____

4. Write only the answers: 99 + 35 = _____   81 − 56 = _____   12 × 4 = _____

7. Central Bank has 67 bags with money. Each bag has 1 thousand dollars. How much money is in the bags?

8. Shade one half.

9. Draw and shade $1\frac{1}{2}$.

10. Apples cost 79¢ a pound and grapes cost $1.45 a pound. What is the total cost of 3 pounds of apples and 4 pounds of grapes?

11. Draw the fourth term and finish the table.

Term	1	2	3	4	5	6	10
Number of Squares	1	___	___	___	___	___	___

19. Write each division problem and answer three ways.

36 ÷ 4 = ___
$\frac{72}{9}$ =
5)‾55

Year End Test, page 2

Name _____

26. Write the next two terms for each pattern.

104	102	100	_____	_____
1	1½	2	_____	_____
21	28	35	_____	_____
$0.70	$0.80	$0.90	_____	_____
25¢	50¢	75¢	_____	_____

36. Jamey is buying candles for a birthday cake for an aunt who is 65 years old. There are 8 candles in a package. How many packages does Jamey need?

38. Draw the hands on the clock to show 5:12.

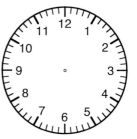

40. 12 × 17 = 204. How much is 12 × 18? _____ Mr. Coles has 204 eggs that he is packing in egg cartons. Twelve eggs fit in a carton. How many cartons does he need? Explain your work.

43. What is the perimeter of a square with a side measuring 29 inches?

45. Add 693 + 5679 + 9650.

47. Subtract 48,537 − 9654.

49. Multiply $6.85 × 37.

Math Journal

Math Journal

Math Journal

Math Journal

Math Journal

Math Journal

Math Journal

Math Journal

Math Journal

Math Journal

Math Journal

Math Journal